Vegetables the Italian Way

Vegetables the Italian Way

by TERESA GILARDI CANDLER

McGraw-Hill Book Company

New York   St. Louis   San Francisco
Düsseldorf   Mexico   Toronto

1 2 3 4 5 6 7 8 9 DODO 8 7 6 5 4 3 2 1 0

LIBRARY OF CONGRESS CATALOGING IN PUBLICATION DATA

Candler, Teresa Gilardi.
Vegetables the Italian way.
Includes indexes.
1.   Cookery (Vegetables)   2.   Cookery, Italian.
I.   Title.
TX801.C32   641.6'5   80-12661
ISBN 0-07-009723-2

Book design by Roberta Rezk

Illustrations by John Murphy

To my husband

2108815

Acknowledgments

Encouragement and support to write this book were found in the delightful association I have had with guests in our home when I was serving food, which I love to do. Their obviously genuine surprise and pleasure at eating vegetables the Italian way gave me the momentum to do the work. For those words of praise, then, I must show my gratitude and say a special thanks to my very dear friend Marian, and to Ros and Bob, Evie and Jules, Gloria and Eugenio, to Lorraine and Joe, and a host of others. *A tutti, grazie!*

And then, when the work really began, I had the efficient help of the lovely Leslie Meredith; to her, and her associates at McGraw-Hill, a thousand thanks!

Contents

Introduction

This book is the result of two experiences of my youth. Early every Saturday morning I would accompany my father to the fruit and vegetable market in my home town of Torino. I watched him select only the very best produce for his restaurant, Belvedere. The market people knew my father well and kept the very best vegetables for his demanding, critical eye. Everything looked so good and so fresh. Later, I would watch the chefs prepare the beautiful dishes served at Belvedere.

Soon, I was able to put into practice everything I learned, cooking first at my father's restaurant in Italy, and later in America, my adopted country of twenty years. Over the years, I've learned just how to please my family and guests when they sit down at the table—and I've shared many of my secrets with the readers of my food columns. Now I would like to share the secrets I have learned—about serving the best recipes of Italy using the best ingredients of America—with you.

Between these two covers there is something for everyone. Most of the recipes have originated from chefs—and from housewives who are unsung chefs themselves. Many cities, towns, and villages in Italy, from the Alps of Piemonte to the seashores of Sicilia, are represented. From these regions I get my inspiration, which I apply in these recipes for vegetables native to or available in America.

Each region of Italy has its own special way of cooking vegetables. Sometimes this may be confusing since each area may also have its own name for a dish which is common to all parts of the country. (If you are traveling in Italy you have to remember this fact.) Most of the recipes are traditional, besides being regional; others have been developed by me through years of experimentation here in my adopted country. This book gives you the tasty results from both countries.

In my new home, I have tried, used, and come to love the many vegetables unknown to me when I first arrived here—kale, for instance, and a type of squash called spaghetti squash, which I learned of only in recent years and which is still unfamiliar to most Americans. In fact, I have found that most Americans limit their vegetable eating to potatoes, green beans, peas, and carrots. What a shame! By doing so, they are not only missing the health value of eating other vegetables, but are also missing the great pleasure, adventure, and surprises of trying new ones.

What is so different about *Vegetables the Italian Way?* In Italy, vegetables appear on the table at every meal, at home or at a restaurant. They are served as an accompaniment to meat, fish, and poultry dishes; they can serve as a separate course; and as hors d'oeuvres or antipasto, young broad beans, red, yellow, and green peppers are unsurpassable. Artichokes, fennels, and mushrooms, to name a few, are often eaten raw. Many vegetables are fried; others are blended with cheeses, sauces, or with rice or pasta, to create the marvelous variety of *timballi, crostate,* and *tortine*. Even at breakfast, when tomatoes are in season, it is not unusual to have for that meal a ripe tomato, sliced, sprinkled with some oil, salt, and pepper. With a slice of crusty Italian bread, I guarantee you would enjoy it too. *Vegetables the Italian Way* will teach you about these and other options for serving American vegetables with an Italian touch at any meal.

Vegetable soups can be made a thousand ways. You may not be familiar with *vellutate di verdura* or *passati di verdura* and may want to try my recipes for these traditional Italian soups after reading how simple they are to prepare. Though many of the vegetables in this book will be familiar to you, they are used in a way you've probably never heard of, let alone tried.

Speaking of soups, the water in which the vegetables are cooked should never be thrown away. If any meat juice or leftover vegetables remain after cooking, Italian women practice what most American housewives do not—economy, with nutrition added—for they save and reuse water and juices that have been enriched by the seepage of vitamins from the vegetables into the cooking fluids. I am convinced that we in this country have the best-fed sinks in the entire world!

Until the day I landed in the United States, I did not know of any vegetables except the garden-fresh or pickled variety. In Italy, the choice of produce was decided by the season. Very few vegetables were commercially canned, and cans were never available to me. (That tells a little about my age, I'm afraid.) Some housewives would pickle a vegetable to preserve it so that they could enjoy it with their families in the off-season days. I include many recipes with which you can do this too.

Collecting the recipes for this book took a long time, but doing so and writing about them has been a challenging and exciting experience for me—enjoyable and satisfying at the same time. I hope that it will be the same for you, every time you use this cookbook. Have fun, and *buon appetito!*

II
Some Thoughts and Suggestions

Vegetables should be included in meals every day, to insure an adequate intake of essential nutrients. Always buy fresh vegetables in quantities that can be used in just a few days. Make certain that they are stored and cooked properly to conserve the nutritive value, the flavor, and the texture.

If you prefer to wash fresh vegetables before you store them, they should then be dried well, placed in a plastic bag or tight-fitting container, and stored in the crisper of the refrigerator. This helps to conserve some vitamins, such as vitamin C, otherwise easily destroyed by exposure to air.

You may store fresh vegetables in the refrigerator for three to five days, no longer.

On the matter of fresh versus frozen vegetables: if it is impractical for you to make frequent trips to the market for fresh vegetables because of your busy life, traveling distance, and so on, you may want to take advantage of frozen vegetables. For this reason, when appropriate, I give you a choice of fresh or frozen vegetables.

Very often frozen vegetables are higher in nutritive value than their fresh counterparts. Because frozen vegetables have been picked at the peak of their quality, then transported immediately to a nearby processing plant to be blanched and quickly frozen, they retain much of their original nutritional value. The time needed to transport fresh vegetables to distant markets often results in some loss of nutrients.

Frozen vegetables should be kept frozen by storing in the

freezer at zero degrees Fahrenheit, or lower. Check freezer temperature with a freezer thermometer if you want to be sure. Or, if your freezer cannot keep ice cream brick-solid, the temperature is above the recommended level for any but very short-term storage.

Often in my recipes I call for canned plum tomatoes. The reason for this is very simple: they taste better than the fresh tomatoes you will find most of the time in the markets. Of course, if you have your own garden, or a farmer next door, nothing beats a fresh-picked, sun-ripened tomato.

Imported dried mushrooms are very good, even if very expensive; but a few of them added to the fresh white mushrooms available in our markets do wonders for a dish. Always soak dried mushrooms in cold water for thirty minutes before using; reserve the water; rinse the mushrooms, chop, and add to fresh mushrooms. Filter the reserved water, and use in sauces, gravy, or in any recipe that calls for mushrooms.

You should also know about an Oriental mushroom, called "Shiitake" (see Vegetable Glossary). It is a very good substitute for the Italian and French imported porcini, but much less expensive.

Several recipes call for anchovies. If you feel that anchovies are too salty for your taste, soak them in cold water for fifteen minutes, pat dry, and use. Most of the salt will be gone.

Again, on the subject of salt; if you have to omit salt from recipes for health reasons, substitute herbs. If herbs are called for in the recipe already, plus, say, one teaspoon of salt, substitute for the salt one-quarter teaspoon (additional) of herbs. If no herbs are in the recipe, but the recipe requires, say, one teaspoon of salt, substitute for the salt one-half teaspoon of herbs.

There is nothing better than having your own herb garden, with a plentiful supply of fresh herbs. Unfortunately, though, I don't have one (too many rabbits, raccoons, and groundhogs!). Sometimes I can get fresh herbs from a kind neighbor who grows many herbs, including basil, amid his grapes. I am sure that I have more Pesto sauce in my freezer than any family in Genoa!

To freeze herbs, I wash them very thoroughly, spin dry in a salad dryer, then transfer them to plastic bags; they keep their flavor very well.

There are some preliminary preparations of vegetables that can be of help since they are good time-savers:

If you want to save parsley for ready use, chop a large amount and keep it in the freezer. The ice tray works very well for this. Place chopped parsley in each compartment, fill with water, and freeze.

To have a vegetable base for roasts and sauces, again, chop a large amount of carrots, celery, and onions; place in small containers and freeze. They will be ready when you're in a hurry and need them quickly.

Do you want to keep asparagus fresh a few days longer? Place the stem bottoms in cold water, then refrigerate.

As to shopping for some of the complements to vegetables, I have a thought or two for you about cheese. Considering the soaring prices of imported cheese, you may want to try available substitutions. As a very good stand-in for Parmesan, you should try the Wisconsin Asiago cheese. A good domestic Swiss cheese can very well take the place of imported Gruyère or Swiss products. And when a recipe calls for Fontina, you could try an American substitute called "Fontinella"; true, it does not give you the full flavor of the Italian Alps, but it makes a highly satisfactory compromise.

As to oil, when it is necessary for flavor I use olive oil. Otherwise corn oil serves the purpose most of the time.

In the case of butter, the reasons for using sweet butter are that it has a better flavor and it is always fresher than salted butter.

You might check your pepper supply. It does not take much more time to grind fresh pepper than it takes to shake a jar of already-ground pepper; but there is a world of difference in the results.

Everyone knows how delicious the homemade beef or chicken broths are; not many of us have them ready in the refrigerator or freezer. Fortunately, our supermarkets have a large variety of very good canned broths. These can be used most satisfactorily. Remember, of course, to remove any fat from either broth before using.

I am often asked if raw vegetables are more nutritious than cooked vegetables. It's true that some nutrients are lost during the cooking process, but it is also true that cooking makes some vegetables more readily digestible, making more of the nutrients available to the body. In any event, vegetables, when cooked properly, still provide very meaningful amounts of vitamins and minerals.

With any herbs that are used to flavor a recipe, it is better to add them during the last minutes of cooking. That way the flavor is not cooked out.

Cook vegetables in as little liquid, and for the shortest time, possible. I prefer to steam vegetables with a minimum of water in a large saucepan. For leafy vegetables such as spinach, don't use any water at all. The water remaining in the leaves after washing them is sufficient.

If you must boil a vegetable, bring the water to a boil before putting the vegetable in the saucepan. This will help save important vitamins.

When I say discard outer, tough leaves from lettuce, endive, and such, I don't mean that you should throw them away. Save all the leaves and make a fast, delicious soup; another good soup is made with fresh pea pods. So, as you look through my book, before you run for the garbage to dispose of the "discards," stop! I am sure you will find many good ways to use leaves, parings, and so on, that you might otherwise have felt inclined to throw away.

In the same vein of thought, keep the leaves from celery. Wash them, spin or pat dry, and place in plastic bags. Chop and add some to your next salad, soup, or stew; you will love the added flavor.

Another "discard," the green leaves from beets, are good added to lettuce, or cooked like spinach.

I much prefer to use "do's" than "don'ts," but if I may be permitted just this one exception, I would urge you: don't add sugar to cooking tomatoes; it will not give them that desirable sun-ripened flavor, but instead will result in an unnatural sweet taste.

Do you cry when you chop onions? Put onions in the freezer for ten minutes, and then chop. It helps.

Some people, in fact many people, keep asking me, "What herbs go with what vegetables?" Here is a list of herbs that can be used successfully with vegetables: basil, marjoram, oregano, rosemary, sage, tarragon, thyme, chives, celery, caraway, and dill seeds; and of course, you can use mint.

If you do not steam your vegetables, but cook them in water instead, save the water. At a later time (but no more than a few days later) you can use it for soups, stews, or sauces, or you can cook rice or pasta in it. For any recipe that calls for broth, it is smart and thrifty to get extra nutrients "free."

If you must reheat cooked vegetables, do it in a double boiler.

Cooked carrots can be added to mashed potatoes; and any cooked vegetable can be chopped and added to ground meat for a meat loaf. Add a few tablespoons of wheat germ if the mixture seems too moist. I think that's a good tip, if I do say so myself.

You may add chopped, cooked vegetables to any gravy; it will only improve the taste.

As I try to convey ideas to you that have been very successful for me, I would like to leave this section on a high note. I suggest you spend some time on the subject of *frittate* (Chapter 7, Main Dishes—Eggs). I promise you will not be disappointed. Not only can you use fresh vegetables for frittate, you can also use cooked, leftover vegetables.

Also, I hope that you will not be disturbed by the fact that I repeat the method of making a frittata in most recipes. I have a good reason for doing it. Like many of the readers of my weekly column, particularly my friends in the expatriate "Fiat fraternity," I personally get frustrated when I am reading a recipe in a cookbook that tells me to look at another recipe for the method of proceeding.

Don't give up on making a frittata, if for health reasons you cannot eat eggs. I have made several frittatas very successfully using any of the frozen egg substitutes.

In my home, frittate are so popular I think soon it will be necessary to write a cookbook just for them.

Now here are some additional thoughts and suggestions for low-calorie vegetable meals and parties:

Low-Calorie Recipes

Marinated artichoke hearts
Pickled asparagus
Onion and anchovy salad
Baked peppers with anchovies
Cabbage soup
Most of the cream soups, if you use the substitute given instead of light cream
Lettuce soup
Squash and rice soup
Vegetable soup with chicken
Raw cauliflower and rice salad
Spinach and meat loaf
Sautéed *scaloppine* with tomatoes
Asparagus with chicken
Romaine lettuce leaves, stuffed with chicken
Artichokes with fillet of sole
Peppers and eggs casserole
Broccoli mold
Mushroom mold
Artichokes with parsley and garlic
Asparagus with mustard sauce
Beet mold with mushrooms
Cardoon in tomato sauce
Baked carrots with lemon
Pan-fried cauliflower
Baked fennel
Kale with tomatoes
Peperonata
Stuffed baked tomatoes
Turnips with lemon sauce

Cucumber salad
Stuffed artichoke hearts
Leeks with caper sauce
Pickled green onions
Soybean sprouts stuffed mushrooms
Cabbage and turnip soup
Cold cucumber soup
Escarole with rice soup
Fennel soup
Spinach soup
Fresh tomato soup *alla Torinese*
Most of the vegetable sauces
Veal stew with small onions
Artichokes with chicken
Celery, carrots, and chicken
Carrot and chicken stew
Peppers and chicken
Fillet of sole with mushrooms
Stuffed zucchini *alla Piemontese*
Artichokes sweet and sour
Asparagus with anchovy sauce
Green beans with anise seeds
Sautéed broccoli with soybean sprouts
Carrots with cinnamon
Celery root with tarragon sauce
Stir-fry kale
Stuffed baked tomatoes
Turnip and carrot puree
Cooked celery root salad

Great Ideas for Vegetable Parties

Bagna Caôda Party: Prepare plenty of fresh vegetables, precut into bite-size pieces, plus plenty of Bagna Caôda (Hot Anchovy-Garlic Dip) and plenty of good bread. I can and do assure you that you and your guests will have a feast to remember.

Frittate Party: A frittate party will also be easy on you because you may prepare the frittate early in the day and serve them at room temperature— providing that your party will not be held in the middle of winter. With various frittate (I serve as many as six different kinds) all you need to add is a good tossed salad. Remember to precut each frittata into twelve wedges so that every guest may have more than one or two kinds without feeling guilty.

Raw-Vegetables-with-Sauces Party: Prepare baskets full of any fresh vegetable that can be eaten raw (almost every vegetable is good raw); precut into bite-size pieces. Have individual salad bowls on the table, as many bowls as you have guests. Prepare large bowls of green mayonnaise; sweet and sour sauce; olive oil, salt, and pepper.

Ask your guests to help themselves. Don't forget baskets of good bread on the table. All you need after this feast is dessert, and a cup of good coffee.

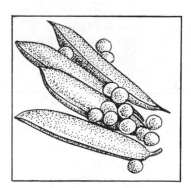

III
Vegetable Glossary

Abbreviations used in the glossary are: g—grams; mg—milligrams; and IU—international units.

ARTICHOKE: The globe artichoke is the unopened bud of a thistlelike plant, native of the Mediterranean countries. Produced here, primarily in California, artichokes are available most of the year, with peak season from April through May. Choose compact, heavy, plump globes, which have tightly closed and fleshy leaves.

Three-and-a-half ounces (100 g) of raw artichokes have only 44 calories; 3 g protein, some fat, 9 g carbohydrate, 51 mg calcium.

ASPARAGUS: A member of the lily family, the asparagus was known in ancient Greece and ancient Rome. Today we may have it from February through June; the main producers are California, New Jersey, and Michigan. Only the green portion of fresh asparagus is tender, so when you buy it, select stalks with the larger amount of green. Stalks should be fresh, firm, and with closed tips; open tips are a sign of overripened asparagus.

Three-and-a-half ounces (100 g) of fresh raw asparagus have only 25 calories; 2 g protein, trace of fat, 3 g carbohydrate, 560 IU vitamin A, 18 mg vitamin C, 2 mg iron, and 200 mg potassium.

References for calories and nutrient content of vegetables were: United States Department of Agriculture; United States Food and Drug Administration; and United Fresh Fruit and Vegetables Association.

GREEN AND WAX BEANS: Of all the varieties of beans, the green and wax beans seem to be the ones mostly used fresh. They are available year-round; the largest producers are California, New Jersey, and Michigan. Fresh green beans should be young and bright in color, stringless, and tender; they should break with a snap, which is why many times they are called "snap" beans.

Three-and-a-half ounces (100 g) of fresh raw beans have only 25 calories; 2 g protein, trace of fat, 7 g carbohydrate, 680 IU of vitamin A, 15 mg vitamin C, 63 mg calcium, 8 mg iron, 170 mg potassium.

DRIED BEANS: This is a broad term for any dried beans that includes the following: kidney beans, pinto, Great Northern, cranberry beans, black-eyed peas, and navy beans. Beans are inexpensive and very nutritious. One pound of dried beans will give you, after soaking, seven to eight cups of beans. They are cholesterol free.

One cup dried, cooked beans contains 210 calories; 14 g protein, 1 g fat, 36 g carbohydrate, 4.3 mg iron, 740 mg potassium, some vitamins B_1, B_2, and B_3.

BEAN SPROUTS: Bean sprouts, the sprouts or shoots of the soya or mung beans, were used in China for thousands of years. They are available in sprout form or can be easily sprouted at home. I had my husband perforate the metal cap of a jar, which then could be used as a "sprouter" with very good results. Just follow the directions on any package of seeds. If you buy them ready to use, do not keep them too long in the refrigerator; they are at their best when very fresh.

Three-and-a-half ounces (100 g) of raw bean sprouts have about 35 calories; 4 g protein, trace of fat, 7 g carbohydrate, 21 mg calcium, 1.4 mg iron, 230 mg potassium, 20 IU vitamin A, and 20 mg vitamin C.

BEETS: These are the red edible root of a biennial plant of the goosefoot family. There are several kinds of beets, but the most popular are red beets. Beets are available year-round and are grown mostly in California, Texas, Ohio, New Jersey, and Colorado. Many times beets are sold with their green leaves attached; the leaves are also quite good (see Some Thoughts and Suggestions). Choose small to medium-size beets, ones that are firm and of good color. Large beets could be woody.

Three-and-a-half ounces (100 g) of raw beets have 30 calories; 1 g protein, trace of fat, 7 g carbohydrate, 6 mg vitamin C, 14 mg calcium, .5 mg iron, 350 mg potassium.

BELGIAN ENDIVE: These thin, elongated stalks, usually bleached while growing, are available from September through May. Many of the ones we use are imported. Try to buy the tightly closed endives, those that are crisp and firm. Very good raw or cooked.

Not too many nutrients are found in Belgian endive, but it also is so low in calories that it makes a delightful alternative for dieters.

BROCCOLI: A member of the cabbage family and a close relative of the cauliflower, it is a native, like so many other vegetables, of the Mediterranean countries and Asia. It is available all year, with the greatest abundance from October to May. California is the largest producer, followed by Texas, New Jersey, Oregon, Florida, and Pennsylvania. When you buy it, it should be dark green or purple green, with closed clusters that have not opened to show the yellow flowers. Stems should not be too thick or it will be tough.

One stalk of raw broccoli or approximately 6 ounces (180 g), has about 45 calories; 6 g protein, 1 g fat, 8 g carbohydrate, 4,500 IU vitamin A, 142 mg vitamin C, 158 mg calcium.

BRUSSELS SPROUTS: Another member of the cabbage family, they look like a miniature cabbage head or a number of cabbage heads attached to a tall stem. Most of the time when you buy brussels sprouts, they have been cut off the stem and placed in small boxes. Good sprouts are firm, compact, and a fresh, bright green. Available most of the year, their peak season is from October through December. The largest growers are California, New York, and Oregon; some are imported.

Three-and-a-half ounces (100 g) of raw sprouts have about 35 calories; 6 g protein, trace of fat, 7 g carbohydrate, 450 IU vitamin A, 80 mg vitamin C, 60 mg calcium, and 380 mg potassium.

CABBAGE: Three major groups of cabbage are available—smooth-leaf green cabbage, crinkly-leaf green Savoy cabbage, and red cabbage. All types may be used for any purpose; they are available all year, with California, Texas, and Florida providing most of the cabbage used in this country. When you buy cabbages, look for solid and heavy heads, closely trimmed, with no loose leaves. Green cabbage is more nutritious than white.

Three-and-a-half ounces (100 g) of raw cabbage have only 20 calories; 1 g protein, trace of fat, 5 g carbohydrate, 48 mg vitamin C, 64 mg calcium, 210 mg potassium, and 180 IU vitamin A.

CARDOON: The cardoon is a cousin of the artichoke, and I believe it to be a second cousin to the celery family. It looks like a giant celery with the prickly leaves of an artichoke. It is little known in America, but is gradually making its way into the American kitchen.

Three-and-a-half ounces (100 g) of raw cardoon have about 20 calories; 1 g protein, 10 mg vitamin C, 5 g carbohydrate, 45 mg calcium, 409 mg potassium, and 320 IU vitamin A.

CARROTS: These are the long, tapering, orange-colored edible roots of a beautiful green plant related to the Queen Anne's lace family. Carrots are one of the most common vegetables. The largest producers of carrots are California and Texas, although they are grown elsewhere. Freshly harvested carrots are available all year, and when buying them you should look for firm, smooth specimens with a good bright orange color.

Three-and-a-half ounces (100 g) of raw carrots have 42 calories; 1 g protein, trace of fat, 10 g carbohydrate, 12,220 IU vitamin A, 40 mg calcium, 9 mg vitamin C, and 375 mg potassium.

CAULIFLOWER: This is the white, edible head formed by the young flowers of a plant in the cabbage family. Cauliflower is available all year, with the peak season from September through January. Look for white to creamy-white, compact, solid heads. Spread-out flowerets are a sign of an overripened cauliflower. California, Oregon, New York, Texas, and Michigan are the major growers.

Three-and-a-half ounces (100 g) of raw cauliflower have 25 calories; 3 g protein, trace of fat, 5 g carbohydrate, 80 mg vitamin C, 29 mg calcium, 1.3 mg iron, 70 IU vitamin A, some vitamins B_1, B_2, and B_3, and 250 mg potassium.

CELERY: Popular and with a thousand uses, celery is available throughout the year. There are two types: the Golden Heart (white) and Pascal (light or dark green). The production is concentrated in California, Florida, Michigan, and New York. When buying celery, look for solid, crisp stalks; avoid wilted celery, with yellow leaves.

Three-and-a-half ounces (100 g) raw celery have 15 calories; 1 g protein, trace of fat, 4 g carbohydrates, 39 mg calcium, .4 g iron, 11 mg vitamin C, 400 mg potassium, and 300 IU vitamin A.

CELERIAC, OR CELERY ROOT: This is often referred to as celery root or celery knob, and is a variety of celery. It should be firm, clean, and unmarked. Originating in the Mediterranean countries, celeriac is now available to us, mainly from California and Florida, from September through May.

Three-and-a-half ounces (100 g) of raw celeriac contain 35 calories; 10 mg vitamin C, some fat, 5 g iron, 38 mg calcium, 1 g protein, and 350 mg potassium.

CUCUMBER: The flavorful fruit of a trailing vine belonging to the gourds family, cucumbers are available throughout the year, produced at various times in many states. The best cucumbers are the dark green-colored ones, which should be very firm over their entire length. Avoid overgrown cucumbers as they are full of seeds.

Three-and-a-half ounces (100 g) of raw cucumbers have 15 calories; 1 g protein, trace of fat, 4 g carbohydrate, 11 mg vitamin C, 17 mg calcium.

CORN: Corn is probably the only native American vegetable. Available all year, it has its best season from May to September. The most readily available is the yellow-kernel corn, although white corn is also common.

Three-and-a-half ounces (100 g) of fresh raw corn kernels have 60 calories; 1 g fat, 2 g protein, 12 g carbohydrate, 2 mg calcium, 69 mg iron, 150 mg potassium, 6 mg vitamin C, and some vitamins B_1, B_2, and B_3.

DANDELION: This is the weed that drives so many homeowners crazy, because of what it does to a green lawn. At the same time, it is a treat for those who have learned how to use it. It can be used raw in a salad or cooked; and for some, it can be used to make wine. Use the young and tender ones for salad, and cook the larger ones.

One hundred grams of raw dandelion have 40 calories; 2 g protein, 1 g fat, 15 mg vitamin C, 7 g carbohydrate, 100 mg calcium, 1.5 mg iron, some vitamins B_1 and B_3, and 11,000 IU vitamin A.

EGGPLANT: One of the best-looking vegetables in the market, eggplants are not used as much as many other vegetables. The most common variety has dark purple skin and a white, spongy flesh. Eggplants are most plentiful during the summer months, but you may find them during the rest of the year, too. Eggplants grow primarily in California, Florida, and Texas.

Three-and-a-half ounces (100 g) of raw eggplant have 19 calories; 1 g protein, trace of fat, 4 g carbohydrate, and 11 mg calcium.

FENNEL: Fennel is of the carrot family, but it does not resemble carrots in shape. It looks like a white bulb, with bright green feathery tops. It is delicious raw, and very good cooked in many different ways. When you buy fennel look for very white, firm bulbs. If you have never had fennel, be prepared for a surprise. Fennel has a very definite anise (licorice) flavor. It is usually available from September to May.

Three-and-a-half ounces (100 g) of raw fennel have 25 calories; 11 g carbohydrate, 35 mg calcium, 8 mg iron, 375 mg potassium, 9 mg vitamin C, and 10,500 IU vitamin A.

JERUSALEM ARTICHOKE: Also known as sunchoke, it is a relative of the sunflower. Available in supermarkets from September to March, it is primarily grown in California.

Three-and-a-half ounces (100 g) of raw Jerusalem artichokes have from 10 to 75 calories, depending on how long a time has elapsed since they were harvested; 1 g protein, trace of fat, and 16 g carbohydrate.

KALE: Kale is the silvery dark-green-leaf vegetable that you see in supermarkets from October to March. It is grown in Florida, southern New Jersey, Virginia, and Maryland and belongs to the cabbage family. Avoid buying any with soft leaves; they should be crisp, almost stiff.

Three-and-a-half ounces (100 g) of raw kale have 45 calories; 5 g protein, 7 g carbohydrate, 200 mg calcium, 1.8 mg iron, 240 mg potassium, 102 mg vitamin C, and 9,000 IU vitamin A.

LEEK: To the new buyer, a leek looks like a giant scallion; it belongs to the same family, but unlike scallions, leeks are expensive. They are grown in California, Texas, Oregon, and the Great Lakes region and are available from September through April.

Three-and-a-half ounces (100 g) of raw leeks have 45 calories; 3 g protein, 10 g carbohydrate, 30 mg calcium, .6 mg iron, 230 mg potassium, and 17 mg vitamin C.

LENTIL: A disc-shaped legume about the size of a half pea, it is used in soups, stews, and even as a base for dips. Lentils are rich in protein and often are used as a meat substitute. They are grown in Washington State and Idaho.

One-half cup (100 g) of dried lentils have 106 calories; 8 g protein, 19 g carbohydrate, .6 mg vitamin B_1, .06 mg vitamin B_2, .07 mg vitamin B_3, 2.1 mg iron, and 153 mg phosphorus.

LETTUCE: There are various kinds of lettuce, even some with red leaves, but the main type is the solid-head kind generally called Iceberg. Among the vegetables available and used most, lettuce is probably the most popular. It is available all through the year; at various seasons it comes from California, Arizona, New York, New Jersey, Texas, New Mexico, Wisconsin, and Colorado. Besides Iceberg lettuce, other types include Boston, Bibb, Butterhead, and romaine.

Three-and-a-half ounces (100 g) of fresh lettuce give you only 15 calories; 1 g protein, trace of fat, 4 g carbohydrate, and 3,000 IU vitamin A.

MUSHROOMS: Regardless of the fact that there are a thousand varieties of wild mushrooms growing in the woods, only one kind can be grown commercially—the white mushrooms you will find in every market, all through the year. They are grown in houses, cellars, and in caves; most come from Pennsylvania, but many are produced in California, New York, and Ohio. When you buy mushrooms, look for very firm white specimens.

Three-and-a-half ounces (100 g) of raw mushrooms have 20 calories, 2 g protein, 3 g carbohydrate, 2.4 mg vitamin B_2, 3 mg vitamin B_3, 7 mg calcium, and 290 mg potassium.

The Shitaki or Shiitake mushrooms from Japan are thick and fleshy with short, two-inch stems and wide brownish caps. Enoki mushrooms have long thin stems and small caps.

ONION: This is the edible bulb of a plant of the lily family; there are several varieties of onion, but the most common is the yellow-skinned Globe onion, used mostly for cooking. Spanish onions resemble the Globe onion in shape, but normally are much larger; they are mild in flavor and often called sweet onions. The red, almost dark burgundy-colored onion is the Bermuda onion, also sweet. The Bermuda and the large yellow Italian imported very sweet onion are excellent for salads. Most onions are grown in California, Texas, Colorado, Oregon and Idaho.

Three-and-a-half ounces (100 g) of raw onion have 35 calories; 2 g protein, trace of fat, 10 g carbohydrate, 30 mg calcium, 12 mg vitamin C, and 120 mg potassium.

PARSNIP: The parsnip is the root of a plant of the same family as carrots and fennels. Grown in the Great Lakes region, California, and Texas, their flavor is not fully developed until after prolonged exposure to low temperatures which changes the starch into sugar. For that reason they have more calories than carrots or fennels. Parsnips must be cold-stored; they are never used directly from the fields.

Three-and-a-half ounces (100 g) of fresh raw parsnips have 75 calories; 2 g protein, 1 g fat, 23 g carbohydrate, 55 mg calcium, 6 mg iron, 450 mg potassium, 30 IU vitamin A, some vitamins B_1, B_2, and B_3, and 12 mg vitamin C.

PEAS: Fresh green peas are rarely seen in the markets any more, because few people care to shell them. Also, peas of high quality are difficult to find. This is because peas must be cooled quickly after harvesting, and kept cool at all times. If allowed to warm, they lose sugar and tenderness quickly. So the best substitute for fresh peas are the fresh frozen peas. Grown in California, Colorado, Washington State, Wisconsin, Minnesota, and New York State, they are available year round.

Three-and-a-half ounces (100 g) of thawed peas have 85 calories; 4 g protein, trace of fat, 9 g carbohydrate, 430 IU vitamin A, 16 mg vitamin C, 1.2 mg iron, and 85 mg potassium.

PEPPERS: Most of the peppers you find in the markets are the sweet green or red peppers. Mainly grown in Florida, they are available all year, but are most abundant from May through October. When you buy peppers, you should always look for those which are fresh, firm, thick-fleshed, and bright in color. Avoid very thin peppers, or peppers that are wilted; they will be bitter.

Three-and-a-half ounces (100 g) of fresh green peppers have 21 calories; the red peppers have 30 calories for the same amount. Both contain 2 g protein, 5 g carbohydrate, 7 mg calcium, 157 mg potassium, 425 IU vitamin A, plus 105 mg vitamin C.

POTATO: A vegetable tuber from a plant of the nightshade family, the principal varieties include: White Rose (long white); Katahdin (round and white, low in starch); Red Pontiac (round red); and Russet Burbank, known all over as the Idaho potato—the best for baking purposes. They are grown in Maine, Idaho, and California. If you refrigerate raw potatoes, the starch content will convert to sugar, just as it does in parsnips.

Three-and-a-half ounces (100 g) of raw potato contain 90 calories; 3 g protein, trace of fat, 22 g carbohydrate, 20 mg vitamin C, 782 mg potassium, 1.1 mg iron, and 14 mg calcium.

PUMPKIN: This is the orange fruit of a trailing vine belonging to the gourd family. It is available from late September through October. For many recipes quite a large number of good brands of canned pumpkin are available.

Three-and-a-half ounces (100 g) of fresh pumpkin have 28 calories; 1 g protein, 10 g carbohydrate, 30 mg calcium, 320 mg potassium, 11,000 IU vitamin A, and 10 mg vitamin C.

RUTABAGA: Rutabaga is of the same family as turnips, though larger than turnips, and with a dark yellow flesh. Rutabagas are higher in total dry matter and total digestible nutrients than turnips.

Three-and-a-half ounces (100 g) of fresh raw rutabagas have 35 calories, 1 g protein, 5 mg carbohydrate, 45 mg calcium, 4 mg iron, 80 IU vitamin A, a little vitamins B_1, B_2, and B_3, plus 42 mg vitamin C.

SPINACH: Always look for stocky plants, with crisp dark green leaves. Spinach is available all year.

Three-and-a-half ounces (100 g) of fresh raw spinach have 28 calories; 4 g protein, 4 g carbohydrate, 4 mg iron, 510 mg potassium, 45 mg vitamin C, and 9,000 IU vitamin A.

SQUASH: The squash is the fruit of a hundred types of vines of the gourd family. Most of the squash is known as summer or winter squash; these are only commercial names, not botanical ones. The most common of the winter squash are: Acorn, Butternut, Buttercup, Hubbard, green and gold Delicious, and Banana squash.

Three-and-a-half ounces (100 g) of fresh, raw winter squash have 60 calories; 2 g protein, trace of fat, 16 mg carbohydrate, 26 mg calcium, 1 g iron, 550 mg potassium, 4,500 IU vitamin A, and 20 mg vitamin C.

The most important varieties of summer squash are: Crookneck, Straightneck, Patty Pan, Marrow, and the well-known zucchini, plus Chayote.

Three-and-a-half ounces (100 g) of fresh, raw summer squash have 15 calories; 1 g protein, trace of fat, 3.5 g carbohydrate, 30 mg calcium, 180 mg potassium, 450 IU vitamin A, a little of vitamins B_1, B_2, and B_3, plus 15 mg vitamin C.

SWEET POTATO: Two types of sweet potato are available all year around, one or the other. One, known as yams, is the most common. Yams have an orange flesh, moist and sweet. The dry sweet potatoes have a lighter flesh, very low in moisture, and they do not keep too long; that is the reason that this kind is slowly disappearing from our markets. Most sweet potatoes are grown in the southern states, in areas from Texas to New Jersey; California is also a heavy producer.

100 g of sweet potato, if baked, has 140 calories; if boiled, 110 calories; 1.9 g protein; 32 mg calcium; 7 mg iron; 25 g carbohydrate, 240 mg potassium; 24 mg vitamin C, a small amount of B_1 and B_2; 9,000 IU vitamin A.

SWISS CHARD: Swiss chard looks like a giant spinach, with a long white, sometimes wide, stem; both parts are very good. You may use Swiss chard as you would spinach.

Three-and-a-half ounces (100 g) of fresh raw Swiss chard, leaves or stalks, have 20 calories; 2 g protein, 4 g calcium, 3 mg iron, 600 mg potassium, 9,500 IU vitamin A, some vitamins B_1, B_2, and B_3, plus 60 mg vitamin C.

TOMATO: The ever popular tomato is available to us year-round; but nothing can surpass fresh ones right out of the garden in the summertime. California, Florida, Texas, and many other states are major producers of tomatoes.

Three-and-a-half ounces (100 g) of fresh raw tomatoes have 20 calories, 1 g protein, 4 g carbohydrate, 15 mg calcium, 6 mg iron, 300 mg potassium, 1,000 IU vitamin A, plus 28 mg vitamin C.

TURNIP: The most popular turnip has white flesh with a purple top; many times it is sold with a green leafy top.

Three-and-a-half ounces (100 g) of turnips have 28 calories; 1 g protein, 6 g carbohydrate, 40 mg calcium, 4 mg iron, 190 mg potassium, a small amount of vitamins B_1, B_2, and B_3, plus 28 mg vitamin C.

1 Preserving, Pickling, Freezing

Conservazione al naturale, sott'aceto, e surgelatura

PRESERVING AND PICKLING
Conservazione

NOTE: When sterilizing and sealing jars, follow the instructions exactly as described by the manufacturer of your commercial preserving jars.

PICKLED ASPARAGUS

Asparagi sott'aceto

May be served as an appetizer.

5	pounds fresh asparagus
¼	cup salt
3	cups white vinegar
1½	cups water
2	teaspoons mustard seed
1	teaspoon black peppercorns
4 to 6	sprigs fresh tarragon, or
4	teaspoons dried tarragon leaves

To prepare fresh asparagus, remove tough ends (saving them to make a soup). Leave the green parts whole and soak in cold water; rinse well. Transfer to a large saucepan and cover with hot water. Add salt and bring to a boil. Boil for 2 to 3 minutes, uncovered.

Very gently remove asparagus from water and place over towel to drain well. Arrange asparagus, tips up, in sterilized jars. Cover.

Bring vinegar, 1½ cups water, mustard seed, and peppercorns to a boil; boil for 2 minutes. Fill the jar with hot liquid, add some tarragon to each jar, and close tight. Store for 3 weeks before using. Makes 5 quart jars.

PICKLED GREEN BEANS
Fagiolini verdi sott'aceto

Good mixed with any leftovers.

 2 pounds fresh green beans
1½ cups white vinegar
1¼ cups water
 4 teaspoons salt
 2 teaspoons mustard seed or dill seed
 2 teaspoons whole peppercorns
 2 cloves garlic, peeled and sliced

Remove ends from beans; wash, drain, set aside.

In a saucepan, combine vinegar, water, salt, mustard seed, peppercorns, and garlic. Bring to a boil, cover, and simmer for 10 minutes.

Pack whole green beans into hot sterilized jars; fill to within ½ inch of top with hot liquid, making sure liquid covers beans. Seal. Process in boiling water for 20 minutes. Makes 3 pints.

PICKLED BEETS
Barbabietole sott'aceto

 5 pounds small beets
 6 cups white or cider vinegar
 2 teaspoons black peppercorns
10 juniper berries
 6 whole cloves
 2 tablespoons dried marjoram
 1 teaspoon salt
½ cup sugar (optional)
 3 large onions, thinly sliced

Wash beets. Boil for 15 minutes in enough water to cover beets. Drain, reserving 2 cups of cooking water. Plunge beets into cold water. Peel and slice.

Heat vinegar with reserved cooking water. Add peppercorns, juniper berries, cloves, marjoram, salt, and sugar. Bring to a boil. Reduce heat and simmer for 5 minutes. Keep hot.

Arrange beets and onions in layers in clean canning jars. Cover with hot vinegar mixture. Seal, cool. Beets will keep in the refrigerator for several weeks. Makes about 8 pints.

PICKLED CARROTS
Carote sott'aceto

3	pounds small fresh carrots
	white wine vinegar or tarragon vinegar
20	fresh basil leaves
16	black peppercorns
4	tablespoons sugar

Scrape carrots; wash; and cut as desired in rounds or strips. Place in vegetable steamer over 1 inch salted water; cover and steam for 8 minutes. Drain. Arrange carrots in hot sterilized jars, in layers with basil leaves and peppercorns. Fill jars with vinegar to within ½ inch of top. Sprinkle some of the sugar in each jar; seal. Shake gently and set in a cool place.

Carrots are not ready to be used until after at least 1 month. You do not need to boil filled jars, because the vinegar will act as a preservative. Makes about 5 pints.

PICKLED CAULIFLOWER
Cavolfiori sott'aceto

4	pounds fresh cauliflower, trimmed
3	tablespoons salt
2	cups white vinegar
1½	cups water
10	bay leaves
4	sprigs tarragon, or
2	teaspoons dried tarragon leaves
2	cloves garlic, sliced
6	whole cloves

Wash cauliflower and break into flowerets. Fill a large pot with water; add salt and bring to a boil. Add cauliflower and boil for 2 minutes. Drain, and rinse with cold water. Taste; if too salty rinse once more with cold water.

Combine vinegar, water, bay leaves, tarragon, garlic and cloves in a saucepan; stir and boil for 5 minutes.

Pack cauliflower in hot sterilized jar, fill to within ½ inch of top with hot liquid, making sure liquid covers cauliflower. Seal. Process in boiling water for 15 minutes. Makes 6 pints.

PICKLED CELERY
Sedani sott'aceto

8   cups sliced celery, outer stalks only
2   cups white wine vinegar
2   cups water
4   cloves garlic, sliced
4   bay leaves, crumbled
8   whole cloves
1   teaspoon salt
1   teaspoon black pepper
10 fresh basil leaves

Trim celery, and remove strings. Place in a large kettle with vinegar, water, garlic, bay leaves, cloves, salt, and pepper. Bring to a boil, and boil for 10 minutes. Remove from heat immediately and pack celery into hot sterilized jars. Fill with liquid from kettle and all the spices. Add basil leaves to each jar. Make sure liquid covers celery. Seal and set in a cool place. Makes about 6 pints.

PICKLED CUCUMBERS
Cetrioli sott'aceto

This quick method gives you very good pickles, but they must be used within three to four weeks.

4   quarts small cucumbers, about 3 to 4 inches long
3   quarts water
3   quarts vinegar
1   cup salt
6   cloves garlic, peeled and sliced
2   teaspoons black peppercorns
1   teaspoon whole cloves
5   bay leaves
2   teaspoons marjoram

Thoroughly wash cucumbers; dry well. Pack into sterilized jars.

Place water, vinegar, salt, garlic, peppercorns, cloves, bay leaves, and marjoram in a large kettle. Bring to a boil; reduce heat, cover, and simmer for 30 minutes. Remove from heat, cool, and pour over the cucumbers, filling the jars to within ½ inch of top. Seal immediately and refrigerate. Makes 4 quarts.

PICKLED EGGPLANTS
Melanzane sott'aceto

4 large eggplants
6 cloves garlic, sliced
1 16-ounce jar pimiento strips
6 teaspoons white peppercorns
6 teaspoons red pepper flakes
6 bay leaves, crushed
6 teaspoons dried marjoram
8 cups white vinegar
2 tablespoons salt

Peel eggplants and dice. Place in vegetable steamer over 1 inch salted water. Cover and steam for 2 minutes. Drain well. Pack into hot sterilized jars. Add to each jar some of the garlic slices, pimiento strips, peppercorns, pepper flakes, bay leaves, and marjoram.

Bring vinegar with salt to a boil. Pour hot over eggplants, filling to within ½ inch of top, making sure liquid covers eggplants. Seal, and keep in a cool place. Makes 6 pints.

PICKLED JERUSALEM ARTICHOKES
Topinambur sott'aceto

5 pounds fresh and firm Jerusalem artichokes
3 quarts water
1 cup salt
6 cups white vinegar
3 cups water
3 cloves garlic, sliced
3 teaspoons mustard seed
1 teaspoon black peppercorns

Scrape artichokes very well with a vegetable brush. Cut into 1-inch cubes and rinse well. Bring to a boil the 3 quarts of water with the salt; boil until salt has dissolved.

Place cubed artichokes in a large bowl and cover them with salted water. Cover bowl and let stand overnight at room temperature. Rinse cubes well, drain, and place into hot, sterilized jars.

In a saucepan combine vinegar, water, garlic, mustard seed, and peppercorns. Bring to a boil, reduce heat, and simmer for 15 minutes. Fill jars to within ½ inch from top with hot liquid, making sure liquid covers artichokes. Seal, and refrigerate at least 24 hours before serving. Will keep in refrigerator for up to 3 weeks.

PICKLED MUSHROOMS
Funghi sott'aceto

5 pounds firm white mushrooms or Shiitake mushrooms
3 lemons
6 cups white wine vinegar
2½ cups water
3 tablespoons salt
12 bay leaves
20 black peppercorns
6 whole cloves
6 cloves garlic, whole
olive oil to fill jars

Remove stems from mushrooms and save for other use. Wash mushroom caps briefly in cold water. Toss them with juice from the lemons.

In a large kettle combine vinegar, water, salt, bay leaves, peppercorns, cloves, and garlic. Bring to a boil; add mushrooms and boil for 5 minutes. Drain; remove and discard garlic.

Pack mushrooms in hot sterilized jars. Fill jars with oil to within ½ inch of top, making sure that mushrooms are covered. Seal, and store in cool place. Allow to age for 4 weeks. Refrigerate after jar is opened. Makes 5 quarts.

PICKLED ONIONS
Cipolline sott'aceto

5 pounds small white onions
5 cups white wine vinegar
2 cups water
1 cup olive oil
10 fresh basil leaves
10 bay leaves
1 tablespoon black peppercorns
6 whole cloves
2 tablespoons salt

Peel onions and place in a large kettle. Add vinegar, water, oil, basil leaves, bay leaves, peppercorns, cloves, and salt. Bring to a boil. Continue boiling uncovered for 4 minutes. Transfer onions and hot liquid into hot sterilized jars. Fill jars to within ½ inch of top, making sure liquid covers onions. Seal. Keep in a cool place. Makes about 5 quarts.

PICKLED PEPPERS
Peperoni sott'aceto

Try these on a sliced hard roll as well as serving them as appetizers.

For every 2 pounds of fresh peppers you need:
1½ cups white wine vinegar
1 cup water
½ teaspoon salt
1 teaspoon black peppercorns
2 bay leaves
18 anchovy fillets, cut in half
garlic to taste
olive oil, enough to fill jars

Use red peppers: they keep better and are sweeter. Wash peppers, place under broiler, and broil until skin begins to bubble. Remove from oven and peel while hot. Cut in half lengthwise and remove seeds and pith. Cut into 1-inch strips.

After the peppers have been broiled, cleaned, and cut into strips, bring vinegar, water, salt, peppercorns, and bay leaves to a boil. Drop peppers into boiling liquid and boil for 2 minutes only—the peppers will get too soft if you leave them longer. Drain immediately and lay peppers flat on a clean surface.

Place half of an anchovy fillet on top of each piece of pepper. Roll up lengthwise and place in sterilized jars. Add sliced garlic among layers of rolled-up peppers. Fill with olive oil to within ½ inch of top, making sure oil covers peppers. Seal, and keep in a cool place. Makes 2 quart jars.

PICKLED GREEN TOMATOES
Pomodori verdi sott'aceto

1 gallon small green tomatoes
6 cloves garlic, sliced
6 stalks celery, cut into 2-inch pieces
6 green peppers, quartered
2 quarts water
1 quart white vinegar
1 cup salt
6 sprigs fresh dill, or
3 teaspoons dry dill
2 teaspoons black peppercorns

Wash tomatoes and pack into hot sterilized jars. Add to each jar some garlic, celery, and green pepper.

In a kettle combine water, vinegar, salt, dill, and peppercorns. Bring to a boil; boil for 5 minutes. Pour hot liquid over tomatoes in jars and fill to within ½ inch of top. Make sure that liquid covers tomatoes. Seal. Process for 5 minutes.

These will be ready for use in 4 to 6 weeks. Makes about 6 quarts.

FREEZING
Surgelatura

The following process may be used for asparagus, green or wax beans, broccoli, brussels sprouts, carrots, cauliflower, and any kind of summer squash.

Wash fresh vegetables and cut into desired length. Place in wire basket or cheesecloth. Bring a kettle of water to a boil; immerse vegetables in it. Begin to count blanching time as soon as vegetables are placed in water. Blanch according to schedule below. Cool immediately under running water, and drain well before transferring to plastic bags. Place in freezer as soon as possible.

	Blanching time
Asparagus	4 minutes
Green or wax beans	3 to 4 minutes
Broccoli	3 to 5 minutes
Brussels sprouts (whole sprouts)	4 minutes
Carrots	3 minutes
Cauliflower flowerets	3 minutes
Summer squash	2 minutes*

*Overblanching will cause squash to become very mushy.

2
Appetizers

Antipasti

Some Suggestions for Appetizers

The following appetizers can be served with cocktails:

> Marinated artichoke hearts
> Carrot and cheese balls
> Eggplant sticks
>
> Stuffed artichoke hearts
> Pickled asparagus
> Carrot and zucchini puffs
>
> Pickled green onions (scallions)
> Soybean sprouts stuffed mushrooms
> Carrot and cheese balls

The following appetizers should be served at the dinner table. Have each portion ready at each place setting. All of these look beautiful served on lettuce leaves:

> Asparagus and prosciutto rolls
> Cold asparagus with tuna fish
> Leeks with caper sauce
> Mushroom and cheese salad
> My father's mushroom salad
> Peas with homemade mayonnaise
> Baked peppers with anchovies

MARINATED ARTICHOKE HEARTS
Carciofi marinati

20 artichokes, the small variety
3 lemons
2 cups dry white wine
3 cups white vinegar, if possible a white wine vinegar
2 teaspoons rosemary leaves
3 cloves garlic, sliced
4 bay leaves
1 teaspoon black peppercorns
1 teaspoon dried marjoram
2 teaspoons salt
  olive oil

To prepare artichokes, hold each by the stem and break off the outer leaves, bending them back until they snap off. With scissors snip off the sharp tip of each leaf and slice off 1 inch from center top of artichoke. Cut in half lengthwise and remove fuzzy choke. Drop into a bowl of cold water to which the juice of the lemons has been added, to prevent artichokes from turning brown.

Drain artichokes and place in a large saucepan, side by side, stems up. Add wine, vinegar, rosemary leaves, garlic, bay leaves, peppercorns, marjoram, and salt. Bring to a boil, lower heat, cover saucepan, and simmer for 20 minutes. Remove from heat and cool artichokes in marinade.

When artichokes are cooled, drain well and put into sterilized canning jars. Cover with oil and close tightly. Check for two or three days to see if oil has been absorbed; add again to cover artichokes. Keep in a cool place; it is not necessary to refrigerate until you open the jar for use. Use within 2 weeks. Makes 2 to 3 quarts.

STUFFED ARTICHOKE HEARTS
Carciofi ripieni

Can be prepared ahead of time and baked at the last minute.

Preheat oven to 500°F
- 5 anchovy fillets, finely chopped
- 1 clove garlic, finely chopped
- 4 sprigs fresh parsley, finely chopped
- 1 tablespoon chopped chives
- 4 tablespoons unflavored bread crumbs
- 4 tablespoons olive oil
- 10 ounces frozen or canned artichoke hearts, defrosted, well drained

Place chopped anchovy fillets, garlic, parsley, and chives in a bowl, add bread crumbs and oil; mix well.

Open artichokes enough to spoon in stuffing; arrange in an oiled baking dish. Bake for 5 minutes. Transfer gently to a serving dish and serve hot. Serves 4 to 6.

RAW ARTICHOKES
Carciofi crudi al pinzimonio

Can be served as an appetizer or in place of a salad.

- 1 medium artichoke per person (for an appetizer one artichoke may serve 2 persons)
- 1 lemon
  olive oil
  salt and pepper to taste

To prepare artichokes see the recipe for Marinated Artichoke Hearts earlier in this chapter. Drop them into a bowl of cold water into which the juice of one lemon has been added, to prevent artichokes from turning brown. Drain very well.

Place a small bowl with olive oil, salt, and pepper in front of each person. Remove one leaf at a time and dip it in oil mixture, eating the white parts only. As you get to the inside you will be able to eat the whole leaf.

Serve this with some good crusty Italian bread and I am sure you will find the combination delightful.

ASPARAGUS AND PROSCIUTTO ROLLS
Rotoli di prosciutto con asparagi

12 asparagus spears—fresh, frozen, or canned—defrosted and well drained
¼ cup olive oil
1 lemon
¼ teaspoon salt
6 slices Italian prosciutto, thinly sliced and cut in half
6 large lettuce leaves
2 hard-cooked eggs, sliced
12 cherry tomatoes

To prepare fresh asparagus, remove the tough ends of stems (reserving them for soup, see Chapter 3), peeling the bottom half toward the tips—or halfway. Soak in cold water and rinse well. Place asparagus in a vegetable steamer or a deep saucepan; cover and cook with 2 inches of salted water for about 10 to 15 minutes, or just until tender. The cooking time depends on size and freshness of asparagus.

Arrange well-drained asparagus in shallow dish. Combine oil, the juice from the lemon, and salt; whisk to mix. Pour over asparagus and marinate in refrigerator for 2 hours. Drain well; wrap each spear with a half slice of prosciutto. Place a leaf of lettuce on each dinner plate, arrange two asparagus rolls on lettuce; decorate with sliced eggs and cherry tomatoes. Serves 6.

COLD ASPARAGUS WITH TUNA FISH
Asparagi freddi con tonno

Can be an appetizer or a main dish for a light summer lunch.

1¼ cups homemade or commercial mayonnaise (For home-made, see Chapter 5, Sauces)
2 pounds fresh asparagus, or
20 ounces frozen or canned asparagus spears, defrosted and well drained
1 6½-ounce can tuna fish, drained
1 small onion
1 teaspoon capers
4 anchovy fillets
6 sprigs fresh parsley

Make mayonnaise and set aside.

To prepare fresh asparagus, see recipe for Asparagus and Prosciutto Rolls in this chapter.

Place tuna, onion, capers, anchovies, and parsley in container of an electric blender or food processor. Cover and process until finely chopped. Add mayonnaise and blend at low speed, until well mixed.

Arrange well-drained asparagus in a deep serving dish; pour mayonnaise mixture over; set aside for 2 hours before serving. Keep in cool place but do not refrigerate. Serves 4 to 6.

PICKLED ASPARAGUS
Asparagi sott'aceto

5	pounds fresh asparagus
¼	cup salt
3	cups white vinegar
1½	cups water
2	teaspoons mustard seed
1	teaspoon black peppercorns
4	sprigs fresh tarragon, or
4	teaspoons dried tarragon leaves

To prepare fresh asparagus, see recipe for Asparagus and Prosciutto Rolls in this chapter. Boil for only 2 to 3 minutes, uncovered.

Very gently remove asparagus from water and place over towel to drain well. Arrange asparagus, tips up, in sterilized jars. Cover.

Bring vinegar, water, mustard seed, and peppercorns to a boil; boil for 2 minutes. Fill the jar with hot liquid, add some tarragon to each jar, and close tight. Store for 3 weeks before using. Makes 5 12-ounce jars.

RAW CARDOON WITH BAGNA CAÔDA
Cardi con Bagna Caôda

A specialty of the Piemonte region of Italy.

3 cardoons, hearts only
2 lemons
1 recipe for Bagna Caôda (see recipe for Hot Anchovy-Garlic Dip, Chapter 5, Sauces)

Cut the tender stalks of cardoons into 1½-inch pieces, removing all strings, if any, as you would with celery. Drop into a bowl of cold water to which the juice of 2 lemons has been added, to prevent cardoons from turning brown. Set aside.

Prepare Bagna Caôda. When sauce is ready, drain cardoons very well. Bring sauce to the table over a burner with a very low flame. Each person dips raw cardoons into the hot sauce. Serve with good Italian or French crusty bread. Serves 6.

RAW CARROT AND CHEESE BALLS
Palline di carote e formaggio

8 ounces cream cheese, at room temperature
1 cup finely grated fresh carrots
1 tablespoon fresh lemon juice
½ teaspoon salt
1 teaspoon white pepper
1 tablespoon finely grated onion
4 tablespoons chopped fresh watercress or parsley

In a bowl, combine cheese, carrots, lemon juice, salt, pepper, and onion; mix well. You may use a blender or food processor, but do not overblend. Place mixture in refrigerator for at least 1 hour. Shape into small balls, and roll in chopped watercress or parsley. Refrigerate until serving time. Serves 6.

CARROT AND ZUCCHINI PUFFS

Bocconcini di carote e zucchine

Bocconcini means little bites. The puffs should be bite-size.

Preheat oven to 375°F.

For the puffs:
- 1 cup hot water
- 8 tablespoons sweet butter or margarine
- ¼ teaspoon salt
- 1 cup flour
- 1½ cups grated fresh carrots
- 4 eggs

For the filling:
- 4 fresh medium carrots, scraped, washed, and diced
- 1 medium zucchini, washed, diced
- ¼ cup hot milk
- 1 tablespoon sweet butter or margarine
- ¼ cup grated Parmesan or Asiago cheese

To prepare puffs, combine water, butter, and salt in a saucepan and bring to a boil. Remove from the heat and add flour all at once. Stir vigorously until mixture forms a ball around spoon. Add carrots; mix well. Mix in eggs, one at a time, and beat until mixture is smooth and shiny. You may use a food processor.

Drop mixture by small teaspoonsful onto a greased baking sheet. Bake in oven for 20 minutes, or until puffs are lightly golden. Remove from oven and cool on wire rack.

To prepare filling, place cleaned and diced carrots in a vegetable steamer with 1 inch salted water. Cover and steam for 15 minutes; add zucchini and steam 10 minutes more.

Transfer to the container of a blender or food processor and puree. Place puree mixture in a bowl; stir in hot milk, butter, and grated cheese; mix well and set aside to cool slightly. Punch a hole in bottom of each puff and, with a pastry bag, fill with carrot filling. Do not refrigerate. Makes about 30 to 40 puffs.

CAULIFLOWER WITH BAGNA CAÔDA

Cavolfiore con Bagna Caôda

Can also be served as a vegetable with broiled fish.

1   cauliflower head, about 1½ pounds
1   recipe Bagna Caôda (see recipe for Hot Anchovy-Garlic Dip, Chapter 5, Sauces)

To prepare cauliflower, remove outer leaves and part of the core. Break into flowerets and place in a vegetable steamer with 1 inch salted water. Steam for 15 to 20 minutes. Drain well and keep warm.

Make Bagna Caôda.

Arrange well-drained cauliflower in a shallow serving dish; pour hot sauce over it, and serve hot. Serves 6.

EGGPLANT FRITTERS

Palline di melanzane

May also be served as a vegetable.

2   medium eggplants
1   egg, beaten
4   tablespoons flour
½   teaspoon salt
¼   teaspoon white pepper
½   clove garlic, minced
1   tablespoon chopped fresh parsley
1   teaspoon baking powder
    oil for frying

Peel and dice eggplant. Place in vegetable steamer with 1 inch salted water. Cover and steam for 10 minutes. Drain and transfer to the container of an electric blender or food processor and puree. Pour into a mixing bowl and add egg, flour, salt, pepper, garlic, parsley, and baking powder. Stir well to blend.

Heat oil in deep fryer. Drop mixture by teaspoonsful to form small balls and fry for 2 minutes or until golden on all sides. Drain on paper towels and serve hot. Serves 6 to 8.

DANDELION SPREAD
Crostini di girasoli

Serve this spread with toasted rounds of bread or on crackers.

½ pound dandelion leaves, or
½ pound watercress or spinach
10 ounces cream cheese, at room temperature
2 teaspoons anchovy paste, or
3 anchovy fillets, finely chopped
¼ teaspoon white pepper

Remove roots and tough stems from dandelions; wash and drain well. Place dandelions, cream cheese, anchovies, and pepper in container of an electric blender or food processor; process until smooth. Transfer to a serving bowl and use as a spread. Makes about 1½ cups.

EGGPLANT STICKS
Bastoncini di melanzane

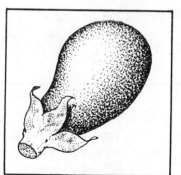

May be served as a vegetable with roast meats.

Preheat broiler.
1 large eggplant, about 1½ pounds
1 cup flour
2 eggs, slightly beaten
½ cup unflavored bread crumbs
½ cup grated Parmesan or Asiago cheese
½ teaspoon white pepper

Peel eggplant and cut in ½-inch-thick slices. Cut each slice into ½-inch sticks. Dip in flour, shake off any excess. Dip first into beaten eggs, then into bread crumbs combined with grated cheese and pepper. Place on a greased baking sheet and broil, about 5 inches from heat, for 5 minutes. Turn over sticks and broil 2 minutes longer, or until golden. Serve hot. Serves 6.

RAW FENNELS
Finocchi in pinzimonio

Serve with crusty Italian bread.

4   medium fennels
1   lemon
    olive oil
    salt and pepper to taste

To prepare fennels, remove and discard tops and tough outer leaves. Cut fennels into 4 wedges and drop in a bowl of cold water to which the juice of the lemon has been added to prevent fennels from turning brown. Drain very well.

In front of each person place a small bowl with some oil, salt, and pepper. Remove one leaf at a time, dipping in oil mixture before eating. Serves 6.

JERUSALEM ARTICHOKES WITH BAGNA CAÔDA
Topinambur con Bagna Caôda

2   pounds fresh and firm Jerusalem artichokes
1   lemon
1   recipe Bagna Caôda (see recipe for Hot Anchovy-Garlic Dip, Chapter 5, Sauces)

Soak artichokes in cold water; scrub very well with a vegetable brush; rinse. Cut into ¼-inch-thick slices and drop in a bowl of cold water to which the juice of the lemon has been added to prevent artichokes from turning brown; leave until serving time.

Prepare Bagna Caôda.

Drain the artichokes and pat dry. Arrange in layers alternating with some of the sauce, and serve warm. Serves 6.

LEEKS WITH CAPER SAUCE
Porri con salsa ai capperi

12   small leeks
5   large lettuce leaves
½   cup finely chopped gherkin pickles
1   tablespoon finely chopped capers
2   anchovy fillets, finely chopped
½   cup olive oil
3   tablespoons wine vinegar

Prepare leeks by trimming off roots and green leaves. Cut in half lengthwise and drop in a bowl of cold water. Let stand for at least 1 hour. Rinse and shake the leeks well to make sure that all the sand has been removed.

Place leeks in vegetable steamer with 1 inch salted water. Cover and steam for 20 minutes, or until fork tender. Drain well. Transfer to a shallow serving dish lined with lettuce. Set aside.

In a small bowl combine pickles, capers, anchovies, oil, and vinegar; beat well with a wire whisk. Pour over leeks and let stand for at least 30 minutes before serving. Serves 6.

MUSHROOM AND CHEESE SALAD
Insalata di funghi a formaggio

1½   pounds large firm white mushrooms or Enoki mushrooms
1   lemon
4   ounces Parmesan or Asiago cheese, slivered
½   cup olive oil
½   teaspoon salt
¼   teaspoon white pepper
2   tablespoons chopped fresh parsley
    lettuce leaves

Wash mushrooms and wipe dry with paper towels; rub well with a lemon slice to keep mushrooms from turning brown. Do not remove stems, but slice very thin lengthwise. Place sliced mushrooms in a bowl; add cheese, oil, salt, pepper, and parsley. Toss gently. Spoon mixture into individual bowls lined with lettuce leaves and place at the table. Serves 6.

MY FATHER'S MUSHROOM SALAD

Insalata di funghi del papá

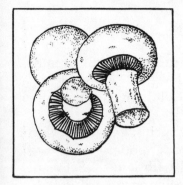

It is doubtful that you can find the *ovoli*, the wild mushroom from Piemonte which was originally used for this salad. Use either white or Enoki mushrooms.

1   pound fresh white mushrooms
1   small white truffle (optional)
2   lemons
½   cup olive oil
3   tablespoons chopped fresh parsley
1   clove garlic, minced
2   hard-cooked eggs, mashed
3   anchovy fillets, chopped
¼   teaspoon white pepper
    salt to taste

Rinse mushrooms and truffle in cold water, without soaking; pat dry with paper towels. Cut into thin slices and transfer to a salad bowl. Sprinkle with the juice from the lemons and toss lightly. This will prevent mushrooms from turning brown.

In another bowl, combine oil, parsley, garlic, eggs, and anchovies; beat well with a wire whisk to mix. Pour over mushrooms, add truffle, shaved; toss lightly. Add pepper, salt for taste. Serve immediately. Serves 6.

ONION AND ANCHOVY SALAD

Insalata di cipolle a acciughe

Serve with Italian bread.

3   large sweet Italian onions, thinly sliced
1   2-ounce can anchovy fillets, with their oil
1   tablespoon capers
4   tablespoons olive oil
2   tablespoons wine vinegar
½   teaspoon black pepper
1   teaspoon dried oregano
3   hard-cooked eggs, diced

Place sliced onions in a salad bowl; dice anchovies and add to onions; top with the capers.

In another bowl, combine oil (also oil from the anchovies) with vinegar, pepper, and oregano; shake well and pour over onion mixture and diced eggs. Toss well and set aside for 30 minutes before serving. Serves 6.

PICKLED GREEN ONIONS (SCALLIONS)
Cipollini sott'aceto

4   bunches green onions
½   cup salt
2   cups white wine vinegar
½   cup olive oil

Remove green tops from onions, leaving about 2 inches of stem above the bulb; remove outer skin. Place onions in a shallow dish; sprinkle salt over them, cover, and refrigerate overnight.

Next day, wash salt off onions; dry with paper towels. Place in hot sterilized jar; combine vinegar and oil in a saucepan and bring to a boil; pour hot liquid over onions in jar. Close jar and allow onions to marinate for at least 3 days before serving. Serves 6 to 8.

PEAS WITH HOMEMADE MAYONNAISE
Piselli con maionese

Serve this with cold meats.

3   pounds fresh peas, or
20   ounces frozen peas
1   cup homemade mayonnaise (see recipe in Chapter 5, Sauces)
    lettuce leaves

If using fresh peas, shell, wash, and place in vegetable steamer with 1 inch salted water. Cover and steam for 8 minutes; drain well. If using frozen peas, thaw; drain well. Peas should be crisp.

Make mayonnaise.

Transfer peas to a salad bowl lined with lettuce leaves; spoon mayonnaise over them; toss gently. Serve at room temperature. Serves 6.

BAKED PEPPERS WITH ANCHOVIES
Peperoni al forno con acciughe

Can be served hot or cold, or in a sandwich.

Preheat oven to 400°F.

3 large green peppers and 3 large red peppers, or
6 green peppers
3 large fresh tomatoes, diced
4 cloves garlic, thinly sliced
12 anchovy fillets, cut into ½-inch pieces
3 tablespoons unflavored bread crumbs
3 tablespoons olive oil
3 tablespoons sweet butter or margarine

To prepare peppers, cut them in half lengthwise; remove seeds and pith; cut into 2-inch-wide strips. Rinse and drain well.

In a bowl, combine tomatoes, garlic, anchovy fillets, bread crumbs, and oil; mix well. Spoon some of the tomato mixture onto each pepper slice; arrange side by side on an oiled baking dish; dot with butter.

Bake, uncovered, for 15 minutes. Serves 6.

ROASTED PEPPERS WITH BAGNA CAÔDA
Peperoni arrostiti con Bagna Caôda

6 green or red medium peppers, broiled, or
16 ounces canned roasted peppers
1 recipe Bagna Caôda (see recipe for Hot Anchovy-Garlic Dip, Chapter 5, Sauces)
4 tablespoons red wine vinegar

Rinse peppers in cold water; gently pat dry with paper towels. Cut into 1½-inch strips, set aside.

Make Bagna Caôda; stir in vinegar.

In shallow serving dish, arrange peppers and sauce in as many layers as possible; finish with sauce. Cover; let stand at room temperature for 2 or 3 hours before serving. Serves 6.

SOYBEAN SPROUTS STUFFED MUSHROOMS
Funghi con germogli di soia

Preheat oven to 350°F.
1   pound fresh mushrooms
1   small onion
1   clove garlic
1   strip bacon
8   ounces lean ground beef
¾   cup soybean sprouts
½   pound Swiss or cheddar cheese, grated
½   cup dry white wine

Wash mushrooms and separate stems from caps. Chop stems and set aside.

Coarsely chop together onion, garlic, and bacon; place in a skillet and stir and cook over medium heat until lightly browned. Add ground beef, stir and cook for 5 minutes; stir in sprouts and chopped mushroom stems. Cook for 5 minutes longer. Add the cheese and wine; stir, raise the heat and cook until wine has evaporated. Remove from heat.

Fill mushroom caps with mixture. Place on a baking sheet. Bake for 15 minutes. Serves 6.

FRIED ZUCCHINI STICKS
Stecchini di zucchine

2   pounds fresh zucchini, each about 6 inches long
1   cup flour
1   teaspoon salt
½   teaspoon white pepper
    corn oil, enough for frying

Do not peel or scrape zucchini, but wash and trim off ends. Cut in half across, then into ½- by 6-inch strips. Combine flour with salt and pepper. Dip zucchini in flour mixture; shake off any excess.

Heat oil in frying pan or deep fryer; drop zucchini a few at a time in hot oil; cook for 2 or 3 minutes, or until golden. Transfer zucchini to wire rack, and keep warm in oven until serving time. They should be nice and crisp. Serves 6.

3

Soups

Zuppe e minestre

CREAMED ARTICHOKE SOUP
Vellutata di carciofi

Can be prepared ahead of time, but the cream should be added just before serving. This soup should be smooth and velvety, for *vellutata* means "like velvet."

4 cups homemade or canned chicken broth
20 ounces frozen or canned artichoke hearts, defrosted and drained
3 tablespoons sweet butter or margarine
3 tablespoons flour
½ teaspoon white pepper
salt to taste
1½ cups light cream, or
1½ cups evaporated milk plus 3 tablespoons nonfat dry milk powder
½ teaspoon thyme
½ cup long grain rice, cooked (optional)

Bring the broth to a boil in a saucepan; add artichoke hearts, cover, and simmer over low heat for 10 minutes. Puree the artichokes with some of the broth in an electric blender or food processor. Return to saucepan with the remaining broth.

Melt butter in a small saucepan, add flour, stir to blend well; stir in cream and thyme. Add pepper and salt. Simmer over low heat for 5 minutes, stirring constantly. Pour cream mixture into the saucepan with broth and artichokes; stir and simmer for 5 minutes. If you add the rice, simmer for 10 minutes. Serves 6.

ASPARAGUS SOUP
Minestra di asparagi

This soup uses the white stalks of asparagus, the parts that are often discarded.

1½ pounds white part only of fresh asparagus
2 tablespoons sweet butter or margarine
2 tablespoons flour
2 teaspoons curry powder
  salt and pepper to taste
4½ cups milk
1 chicken bouillon cube
1 cup small shell macaroni
2 tablespoons fresh chopped parsley

Scrape the white asparagus stalks well; wash and place in saucepan with 3 cups of water and 1 teaspoon salt. Bring to a boil, reduce the heat, cover, and simmer for 45 minutes.

Melt butter in a small saucepan, add flour and curry powder, cook and stir until well blended.

In another saucepan bring the milk to a boil. While stirring, add hot milk all at once to flour mixture. When mixture comes to a boil it will thicken. Reduce heat and simmer for 5 minutes.

Drain asparagus stalks; reserve liquid. Place asparagus stalks in the container of an electric blender or a food processor; blend well. Return to saucepan with liquid, add crushed chicken bouillon cube, milk mixture, and macaroni. Simmer for 10 minutes. Add salt and pepper to taste. Stir in chopped parsley and serve hot. Serves 6 to 8.

ASPARAGUS CREAM SOUP
Vellutata di asparagi

As with most of these "velvety" soups, you may prepare this one ahead of time and add the cream at the last minute.

2	pounds fresh asparagus, or
20	ounces frozen or canned asparagus spears, defrosted
4	cups homemade or canned chicken broth
3	tablespoons sweet butter or margarine
3	tablespoons flour
½	teaspoon white pepper
1	cup light cream, or
1	cup evaporated milk plus 3 tablespoons nonfat dry milk powder
1	tablespoon chopped fresh parsley

To prepare fresh asparagus, see directions in recipe for Asparagus and Prosciutto Rolls, Chapter 2. If using frozen or canned asparagus, cook for only 5 minutes.

Puree the asparagus with some of the broth in an electric blender or food processor. Transfer puree to saucepan with the remaining broth.

Melt butter in a separate saucepan; add flour and blend; stir in pepper and cream. Simmer over low heat for 5 minutes, stirring constantly. Pour cream mixture into saucepan with the puree and broth; stir and simmer for 5 minutes. Sprinkle with the parsley and serve. Serves 6.

2108815

FAVA (BROAD) BEAN SOUP
Minestra di fave fresche

4	tablespoons olive oil
1	large onion, finely chopped
8	ounces canned plum tomatoes, drained and chopped
4	pounds fresh fava beans, shelled
6	cups homemade or canned beef broth
2	cups water
½	teaspoon black pepper
¼	teaspoon nutmeg
12	slices stale whole-wheat bread, ½ inch thick

Heat oil in a large saucepan; add onions and cook until golden. Stir in tomatoes and cook for 5 minutes. Add shelled fava beans, broth, water, pepper, and nutmeg. Bring to a boil; lower the heat, cover, and simmer for 15 minutes, or until beans are soft.

Cut bread slices in half and toast. Place two pieces of toasted bread on bottom of each soup dish; ladle soup over bread, and serve hot. Serves 6.

BEET AND BEAN SOUP

Minestra di barbabietole e fagioli

1	cup dried cranberry beans, or
16	ounces canned cranberry beans, drained
4	tablespoons olive oil
1	medium onion, chopped
1	clove garlic, minced
½	teaspoon dried oregano
6	cups homemade or canned beef broth
2	cups water
2	pounds small beets, peeled and sliced, or
32	ounces canned sliced beets, drained

Wash the beans well in cold water, place in a bowl, and cover with lukewarm water. Set aside to soak overnight.

The following day, heat oil in large saucepan; add onion, garlic, and oregano; stir and cook over medium heat for 5 minutes. Add broth and water. Drain the soaked beans and add to broth mixture. Bring to a boil; lower heat, cover, and simmer for 1 hour. Add beets, cover and simmer for 30 minutes longer. If you are using canned beans, add with beets and cook both only for 30 minutes. Stir in pepper, taste for additional salt, and serve. Serves 6.

GREEN OR WAX BEAN SOUP

Minestra passata di fagiolini

A simple creamed vegetable soup, but unlike *vellutata* soup, cream is never added.

1	pound fresh green or wax beans, or
10	ounces frozen cut green beans, defrosted
2	large potatoes, peeled and diced
8	ounces canned Italian plum tomatoes
¼	cup chopped fresh basil or parsley
3	tablespoons olive oil
1	teaspoon salt
½	teaspoon black pepper
8	cups water
4	ounces small elbow macaroni
½	cup grated Parmesan or Asiago cheese

Remove ends and strings from fresh beans; cut into pieces. Place in a large saucepan. Add potatoes, tomatoes with their juice, basil, oil, salt, and pepper. Add 8 cups hot water; bring to a boil; reduce heat, cover, and gently simmer for 1 hour.

Transfer vegetables with a slotted spoon to the container of an electric blender or a food processor; add 2 cups of liquid from saucepan. Blend until creamy and smooth. Return to saucepan with the liquid; taste for additional salt and pepper.

Add macaroni and cook for 10 minutes. Turn off heat and let stand for 10 minutes before serving. Serve grated cheese in a separate bowl. Serves 6.

BROCCOLI SOUP WITH RICE

Minestra di broccoli e riso

1	bunch fresh broccoli, about 1½ pounds, or
20	ounces frozen broccoli, defrosted and drained
1	cup chopped onions
2	pounds potatoes, peeled and diced
6	cups homemade or canned chicken broth
4	tablespoons sweet butter (optional)
⅓	cup long-grain rice, uncooked
¼	cup grated Parmesan or Asiago cheese
½	teaspoon black pepper
	salt

Discard outer leaves of broccoli. Cut off the lower parts of stalks. Wash and drain. In a large kettle, place broccoli, onions, potatoes, and broth; bring to a boil. Lower heat, cover, and simmer for 1 hour. Transfer all the vegetables to container of an electric blender or food processor and puree. Return to kettle. Add butter and rice; stir, and cook slowly, covered, for 10 to 15 minutes. Rice should be tender but firm. Remove from heat; stir in cheese and pepper; taste for additional salt. Serve hot. Serves 6 to 8.

CABBAGE SOUP WITH RICE

Minestra di cavoli con riso

A Piemontese winter soup.

1 Savoy cabbage, about 1½ pounds, cored and shredded (you may use a food processor for shredding)
4 tablespoons corn oil
1 cup chopped onions
6 cups homemade or canned beef broth
2 pounds potatoes, peeled and diced
⅓ cup long-grain rice, uncooked
½ cup grated Parmesan or Asiago cheese
  salt and pepper to taste

Rinse cabbage well in cold water.

Heat oil in a large pan; add onions and sauté for 5 minutes. Stir in cabbage; reduce heat and cook 5 minutes longer. Add broth and potatoes. Bring to a boil; reduce heat, cover, and simmer for 15 minutes. Transfer all the vegetables to the container of an electric blender or food processor and puree. Return pureed vegetables to pan with broth; add rice; stir, cover, and cook slowly for 12 to 15 minutes. Rice should be tender but firm. Remove from heat, stir in cheese; taste for salt and pepper and serve. Serves 6 to 8.

CABBAGE AND TURNIP SOUP

Minestra di cavolo e rape

10 cups water
1 pound stewing lean beef, cubed
1 pound beef soup bones
1 clove garlic, minced
3 bay leaves
2 tablespoons chopped fresh parsley
6 fresh basil leaves
1 teaspoon salt
½ teaspoon black pepper
1 cup thinly sliced onion
4 large carrots, sliced ¼-inch thick
1 pound Savoy cabbage, coarsely chopped and shredded
3 medium turnips, peeled and diced
3 celery stalks, sliced ½-inch thick
2 large potatoes, peeled and diced
8 ounces fresh green or wax beans, cut into 1-inch pieces
8 ounces canned plum tomatoes, with their juice, chopped
½ cup grated Parmesan or Asiago cheese

Place water in a large kettle; add beef cubes, bones, garlic, bay leaves, parsley, basil, salt, and pepper. Bring to a boil; lower the heat, cover, and simmer for 2 hours, skimming foam as it rises to the surface. Add onions, carrots, cabbage, turnips, celery, potatoes, green beans, and tomatoes. Bring to a boil again; lower the heat, cover, and simmer for 1 hour, or until all the vegetables are cooked. Taste for additional salt and pepper and serve. Serve grated cheese in a separate bowl.

This soup is good hot or at room temperature. Serves 6 to 8.

CARROT SOUP

Minestra passata di carote

8 cups homemade or canned chicken broth
2 pounds fresh carrots, cleaned and diced
2 large potatoes, peeled and diced
½ teaspoon white pepper
3 bay leaves
½ teaspoon rosemary leaves
¼ cup grated Parmesan or Asiago cheese
  salt to taste

Place broth in a large pot; add carrots, potatoes, pepper, bay and rosemary leaves. Bring to a boil; reduce heat immediately, cover, and simmer for 1 hour. Transfer carrots and potatoes to container of an electric blender or food processor and puree. Return pureed vegetables to broth in pot. Stir in grated cheese. Taste for additional salt and serve hot. Serves 6.

CREAM OF CELERY SOUP
Vellutata di sedani

3	tablespoons sweet butter or margarine
2	cups celery stalks, sliced crosswise
1	large leek, washed, cut into ¼-inch slices
2	medium carrots, scraped and diced
4	cups homemade or canned chicken broth
1	cup milk
1	cup light cream, or
1	cup evaporated skim milk plus 2 tablespoons nonfat dry milk powder
1	egg yolk
¼	cup grated Parmesan or Asiago cheese
	salt and pepper to taste

Melt butter in a saucepan; add celery, leek, and carrots. Sauté for 5 minutes. Add broth and milk. Bring to a boil; reduce heat, cover, and simmer for 20 minutes. Transfer vegetables to the container of an electric blender or food processor and puree. Return puree to broth in saucepan.

   Combine cream with egg yolk and grated cheese; mix well. Add, stirring, to soup; taste for salt and pepper and remove immediately from heat. Serve hot. Serves 6.

CHILLED CREAMED CUCUMBER SOUP
Vellutata di cetrioli, fredda

6	large cucumbers
2	medium leeks, sliced crosswise
2	tablespoons butter or margarine
4	cups homemade or canned chicken broth
½	teaspoon white pepper
3	egg yolks
1½	cups plain yogurt or light cream
3	tablespoons chopped fresh basil or parsley mint leaves

Wash cucumbers; cut in half lengthwise and remove seeds. Dice.

Remove wilted leaves from leeks; cut into ¼-inch-thick slices; soak in cold water; rinse very thoroughly. Drain.

Melt butter in saucepan; add sliced leeks and cook until soft; add diced cucumbers, broth, and pepper. Bring to a boil; reduce heat, cover, and simmer for 15 minutes. Transfer cucumber-leek mixture to the container of an electric blender or food processor; cover and puree. Return puree to saucepan with broth; beat in egg yolks, one at a time; simmer for 5 minutes. Remove from heat and chill. Before serving, stir in yogurt and chopped basil. Garnish with a thin slice of cucumber and a mint leaf. Serves 6 to 8.

DANDELION CREAM SOUP
Vellutata di girasoli

Yes, this recipe calls for the dandelions from your lawn, the ones that drive you, me, and many others crazy in the springtime. But here is a recipe that will change your attitude toward this "weed"; you will love the results. It's healthy, too; good hot and excellent cold.

2	pounds fresh dandelions
3	tablespoons sweet butter or margarine
3	tablespoon flour
1	cup light cream, or
1½	cups evaporated milk plus 3 tablespoons nonfat dry milk powder
3	egg yolks
½	teaspoon white pepper
6	cups homemade or canned chicken broth
	salt to taste

Discard any wilted leaves from dandelions. Pull remaining leaves apart from root; rinse well in cold water. Place in vegetable steamer with 1 inch salted water. Cover and steam for 8 minutes. Transfer to the container of an electric blender or food processor and puree. Set aside.

Melt butter in saucepan; add flour; blend well. Stir in cream, egg yolks one at a time, and pepper. Simmer over very low heat for 5 minutes, stirring constantly.

Bring chicken broth to a boil in a large saucepan. Stir in pureed dandelion; reduce heat and stir in cream mixture and continue stirring and simmering for 5 minutes. Serves 6.

ESCAROLE AND PEA SOUP

Minestra di scarola con piselli

1 medium head escarole: use only the green part; save the heart for salad
6 cups homemade or canned chicken broth
2 cups water
10 ounces frozen peas, defrosted
2 tablespoons corn oil
1 medium onion, chopped
½ teaspoon white pepper
   salt to taste
¾ cup very small butterfly macaroni
½ cup grated Parmesan or Asiago cheese

Wash escarole and discard the hard ribs from outer leaves; shred.

In a large kettle combine chicken broth with water. Add escarole and peas. Bring to a boil; reduce heat, cover kettle, and simmer for 15 minutes.

Heat oil in a small skillet. Add onion and pepper and cook until soft. Add to soup in kettle and stir. Add macaroni and cook for 15 minutes. Taste for salt. Serve with grated cheese in a separate bowl. Serves 6.

ESCAROLE SOUP WITH RICE

Minestra di scarola con riso

2 medium heads escarole lettuce (use only the green outer part; save the hearts for salad)
2 tablespoons corn oil
1 medium onion, finely chopped
6 cups homemade or canned chicken broth
2 cups water
½ teaspoon white pepper
¾ cup long-grain rice
½ cup grated Parmesan or Asiago cheese

Wash escarole; remove and discard the hard ribs of outer leaves. Cut remaining leaves into 1-inch-wide strips.

Heat oil in a large kettle. Add onion and cook over medium heat until soft. Add broth, water, pepper, and escarole pieces. Bring to a boil; reduce heat, cover kettle, and simmer for 10 minutes. Stir in rice and continue to simmer for 15 minutes, or until rice is cooked to your liking. Serve hot with sprinkled grated cheese in a separate bowl. Serves 6.

FENNEL SOUP
Minestra passata di finocchi

2 medium fennels
2 medium potatoes
6 cups homemade or canned chicken broth
2 tablespoons white wine vinegar
¼ teaspoon white pepper
    salt to taste

Rinse fennels; remove and discard tops and tough outer leaves. Dice remaining parts. Peel and dice potatoes.

Rinse diced fennels and potatoes well. Place in a saucepan. Add broth and vinegar. Bring to a boil; reduce heat, cover, and simmer for 20 to 30 minutes or until vegetables are soft. Put vegetables into container of an electric blender or food processor and puree. Return to saucepan with broth; stir in pepper; taste for salt. Bring to a boil; remove immediately from heat and serve. Serves 6.

LENTIL SOUP
Minestra di lenticchie

2 pounds pork neck bones
8 cups water
1½ cups dried lentils
3 celery stalks, diced
5 medium carrots, diced
1 large onion, diced
1 teaspoon salt
½ teaspoon black pepper
4 bay leaves

In a large kettle combine all ingredients. Bring to a boil; reduce heat, cover, and simmer for 2 hours. Remove meat from bones; chop and return to the soup. Taste for additional salt and pepper. Serve hot. Serves 6 to 8.

CHILLED LENTIL AND SPINACH SOUP

Minestra fredda di lenticchie e spinaci

1   cup dried lentils
4   cups homemade or canned chicken broth
8   ounces fresh spinach, chopped
2   tablespoons corn oil
1   clove garlic, chopped
1   small onion, chopped
2   cups buttermilk
2   tablespoons chopped fresh or frozen chives
    salt and pepper to taste

Wash lentils and drain. Place with broth in a large saucepan and bring to a boil. Reduce heat, cover, and simmer for 45 minutes. Add rinsed and chopped spinach. Cover and simmer 15 minutes longer.

Heat oil in a small skillet; add garlic and onion. Sauté until onion is soft. Add to lentils in kettle. Transfer all the vegetables to container of a blender or food processor, and puree. Pour into a bowl; add liquid from kettle; stir, cover, and chill overnight.

Remove any fat that has come to the top of soup. Stir in buttermilk and chives; taste for salt and pepper, and serve. (Can be reheated after removing fat in initial chilling.) Serves 6.

LEEK AND POTATO SOUP

Minestra passata di porri e patate

This is excellent served either hot or cold.

4   large leeks
6   cups homemade or canned chicken broth
1½   pound potatoes, peeled and diced
½   teaspoon white pepper
2   tablespoons chopped fresh or frozen chives
      salt to taste

To prepare leeks, trim off the root and cut off green tops. Cut in half lengthwise and drop in a bowl of cold water. Let stand for at least 1 hour. Rinse and shake the leeks well to make sure that all the sand has been removed. Cut into ¼-inch-thick slices, crosswise.

Place leeks in a large kettle with chicken broth, potatoes, and pepper; bring to a boil. Reduce heat, cover, and simmer for 1 hour. Transfer vegetables to a blender or food processor and puree. Return to kettle; add chives; taste for additional salt, stir and simmer for 5 minutes longer. Serves 6 to 8.

LETTUCE SOUP
Minestra di lattuga verde

This is the ideal way of using all of the tough outer leaves of the lettuce you use for a salad.

Remove outer leaves; wash and drain well; pat dry with paper towels. Store in plastic bags and refrigerate for up to five days. You may use curly endive, romaine, or Iceberg lettuce.

3	tablespoons sweet butter or margarine
3	tablespoons flour
6	cups homemade or canned chicken broth
2	cups water
2	celery stalks with leaves, chopped
½	clove garlic, minced
3	cups coarsely chopped lettuce leaves
½	teaspoon white pepper
¼	teaspoon nutmeg
¾	cup long-grain rice, uncooked
½	cup grated Parmesan or Asiago cheese

Melt butter in a large saucepan, stir in flour to form a soft paste. Add broth, water, celery, and garlic; stir well. Bring to a boil; lower the heat, cover, and simmer for 10 minutes. Add lettuce, pepper, nutmeg, and rice; stir well. Cover and simmer 15 minutes longer. Serve hot with grated cheese in a separate bowl. Serves 6.

ONION SOUP WITH WHITE WINE

Minestra di cipolle al vino bianco

4 tablespoons sweet butter or margarine
3 cups thinly sliced onions
½ teaspoon salt
½ teaspoon white pepper
3 tablespoons flour
7 cups homemade or canned beef broth, hot
1 cup dry white wine
12 slices small Italian or French bread, toasted
1 cup grated Gruyère or Swiss cheese

Melt butter in skillet; add onions and sauté over medium heat until golden; sprinkle with salt, pepper, and flour, stir well. Heat broth and white wine in separate saucepan; add to skillet; stir. Cover skillet and cook over low heat for 30 minutes. Taste for additional salt and pepper.

Place 2 slices of toasted bread on the bottom of individual soup bowls; ladle the soup on top of bread and sprinkle with some grated cheese. Serve remaining cheese in a separate bowl. Serve hot. Serves 6.

PEA POD SOUP

Minestra di bacelli di piselli

3 pounds fresh peas with pods
1 large potato, peeled and diced
6 cups homemade or canned beef broth
2 cups water
½ cup finely chopped celery leaves
½ cup long-grain rice, uncooked
½ teaspoon white pepper
½ cup grated Parmesan or Asiago cheese

Shell the peas and use peas for a recipe of your choice. Remove stems from pods, wash carefully, and place in a large saucepan with the diced potatoes, broth, and water. Bring to a boil, lower the heat, cover and simmer over medium heat for 1½ hours. Transfer pea pods and potatoes to the container of an electric blender or food processor, and process until well pureed. Return puree to saucepan, stir in chopped celery leaves, rice and pepper. Cover and simmer for 15 minutes longer. Remove from heat, stir in grated cheese, let stand for 5 minutes and serve. Serves 6.

SPLIT PEA SOUP WITH HAM
Minestra di piselli secchi

3 tablespoons sweet butter or margarine
3 tablespoons corn oil
3 thin slices boiled ham, diced
4 scallions with green tops, thinly sliced
6 cups homemade or canned chicken broth
6 cups water
2 cups dried split peas, very well rinsed
1 teaspoon salt
½ teaspoon white pepper
½ cup grated Parmesan or Asiago cheese

In a small skillet melt butter with oil. Add ham and scallions, cooking over medium heat until golden. Transfer to a large kettle. Add broth, water, peas, salt, and pepper. Bring to a boil; reduce heat, cover kettle, and simmer for 2½ hours. Before serving stir in grated cheese. Serve hot. Serves 6 to 8.

SPINACH SOUP
Minestra di spinaci

Good hot or cold.

2 pounds fresh spinach, washed and chopped
3 tablespoons sweet butter or margarine
1 small leek, white part only, finely chopped
5 cups homemade or canned chicken broth
2 teaspoons arrowroot
2 tablespoons water
1 cup yogurt
  salt and pepper to taste

Wash and chop spinach; do not cook.

Melt butter in a saucepan; add leek and cook over low heat until soft. Add spinach; stir and cook for 4 minutes. Transfer spinach and leek to a blender or food processor and puree. Return to saucepan; add broth. Bring to a slow boil. Dissolve arrowroot in 2 tablespoons cold water; stir into boiling broth. Reduce heat, cook and stir until soup begins to thicken. Remove from heat, and if you serve it hot, stir in the yogurt; taste for additional salt and pepper. If you serve it cold refrigerate to chill and stir in yogurt just before serving. Serves 6.

SQUASH AND SPAGHETTI SOUP WITH MILK
Minestra di zucca al latte

3 pounds Butternut squash or pumpkin
4 cups milk
2 cups homemade or canned chicken broth
8 ounces very thin spaghetti, broken into 2-inch pieces
¼ teaspoon nutmeg
  salt to taste

Peel, seed, and slice squash.

Place squash in vegetable steamer with 1 inch salted water. Cover and steam for 10 to 15 minutes, or until squash is fork tender. Drain and dice.

Combine milk and broth in a kettle; add squash; simmer for 15 minutes. With a slotted spoon; transfer half of the squash from kettle to a blender or food processor and puree. Return to kettle; add spaghetti and nutmeg. Bring to a boil; reduce heat and simmer uncovered for 10 minutes. Taste for additional salt, then serve piping hot. Serves 6.

FRESH TOMATO SOUP ALLA TORINESE

Minestra di pomodori freschi alla Torinese

1	pound sun-ripened tomatoes, or
1	16-ounce can chopped plum tomatoes, with its juice
1	clove garlic
4 or 5	fresh basil leaves
1	tablespoon fresh lemon juice
1	tablespoon sugar
1	teaspoon salt
¼	teaspoon white pepper
2	tablespoons butter
2	tablespoons flour
4	cups heated homemade or canned chicken broth

In a saucepan combine tomatoes with their juice, garlic, basil, lemon juice, sugar, salt, and pepper; cover and bring to a boil. Lower heat and simmer 30 minutes. Pour into blender container or food processor and puree.

Melt butter in same saucepan; blend in flour. Gradually add chicken broth, stirring constantly. Cover and cook over low heat for 10 minutes. Add tomato puree to broth, cook over low heat 10 minutes longer. Serve hot or thoroughly chilled. Serves 6.

TURNIP AND BEAN SOUP

Minestra di rape e fagioli

1	beef or pork soup bone, about 1½ pounds
8	cups water
1	cup dried Great Northern white beans, soaked overnight
2	pounds white turnips, peeled and diced
2	teaspoons salt
½	teaspoon black pepper
2	cups crumbled stale whole-wheat bread

Place soup bone in a kettle with water; bring to a boil. Reduce heat, cover, and simmer for 2 hours. Remove meat from bone and discard bone. Chop meat and return to kettle; add beans, turnips, salt, and pepper. Cover and simmer for 1 hour. Uncover and simmer 30 minutes longer. Stir in crumbled bread; taste for additional salt and pepper and serve piping hot. Serves 6 to 8.

VEGETABLE SOUP WITH CHICKEN

Minestra di verdure con pollo

8   cups water
1   3-pound broiler chicken, cut up
1   large onion, finely chopped
4   celery stalks with leaves, chopped
3   large carrots, diced
3   medium turnips, peeled and diced
16 ounces canned plum tomatoes, with their juice, chopped
3   bay leaves
4   whole peppercorns
1   teaspoon salt
2   tablespoons chopped fresh parsley
½   cup long-grain rice
½   cup grated Parmesan or Asiago cheese

Place water in a large kettle; add cut-up chicken, onion, celery, carrots, turnips, tomatoes, bay leaves, peppercorns, and salt. Bring to a boil; lower the heat, cover and simmer for 1½ hours. Remove from heat, remove skin and bones from chicken, and dice the meat. Set aside.

Transfer the vegetables with a little broth into the container of an electric blender or food processor and puree. Return pureed vegetables to broth in kettle, stir in diced chicken, add parsley and rice; stir. Cover and simmer for 15 minutes. Stir in grated cheese and serve. Serves 6

ZUCCHINI SOUP

Vellutata di zucchine

This soup is equally good hot or chilled—try it both ways.

8   fresh zucchini, about 7 inches long
2   medium onions, chopped
2   teaspoons chopped fresh tarragon leaves or chives
1   teaspoon salt
½   teaspoon white pepper
5   cups homemade or canned chicken broth
1½   cups light cream or
1½   cups milk plus 5 tablespoons nonfat dry milk powder

Wash zucchini; remove both ends and discard. Dice.

In a large saucepan combine diced zucchini, onion, tarragon, salt, pepper, and broth. Bring to a boil. Reduce heat, cover and simmer until onions are tender, about 15 to 20 minutes. Transfer vegetables with a slotted spoon into the container of a blender or food processor and puree. Return pureed zucchini to saucepan with broth. Add cream and warm up over very low heat, stirring constantly. If serving cold, stir in cream at the last minute before serving. Taste for additional salt and pepper. Serves 6.

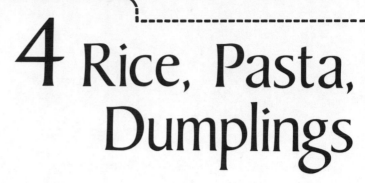

4 Rice, Pasta, Dumplings

Riso, pasta, gnocchi

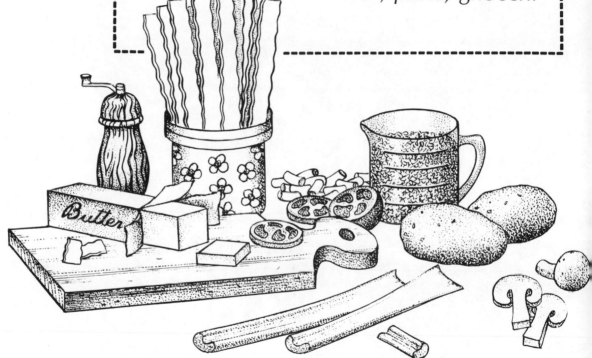

RICE
Riso

RICE WITH ARTICHOKE SAUCE

Riso con salsa di carciofi

This sauce can be prepared ahead of time. At the last minute all you will need to do is cook the rice. Can be kept, without freezing, in a refrigerator for a few days.

6 large artichokes
1 lemon
2 tablespoons butter
2 cups homemade or canned chicken broth
½ cup light cream, or
1 cup low-fat yogurt plus 2 tablespoons nonfat dry milk powder
½ cup grated Parmesan or Asiago cheese
1½ cups long-grain rice, boiled or steamed, or brown rice cooked for 45 minutes

To prepare artichokes, see directions in recipe for Marinated Artichoke Hearts, Chapter 2. Before placing in bowl with lemon juice, cut each artichoke into 4 wedges and each wedge into ¼-inch-thick slices, lengthwise.

Heat broth. In separate heavy skillet, melt butter. Add well-drained artichokes and sauté for 5 minutes. Add hot broth. Cover, lower heat, and simmer for 40 minutes. Transfer artichoke pieces with a slotted spoon to the container of an electric blender or food processor. Add ½ cup of the broth, blend for 2 minutes. Add cream, Parmesan cheese, and blend 2 more minutes or until sauce is smooth. Before using it, pour sauce through a strainer into top of double boiler, over 1 inch of simmering water, and warm.

Place cooked rice in serving dish, spoon some of the sauce over top; serve remaining sauce in separate bowl. Serves 6.

RICE WITH ARTICHOKES
Risotto con carciofi

May also be served as a main dish if accompanied by a vegetable. Good with broiled chicken.

3	medium artichokes
1	lemon
6	sprigs fresh parsley, finely chopped
1	clove garlic, finely chopped
8	ounces cooked ham, finely chopped
2	tablespoons corn oil
½	teaspoon white pepper
4	tablespoons sweet butter or margarine
1	small onion, thinly sliced
1½	cups Arborio Italian or long-grain rice
2	cups homemade or canned chicken broth
2	cups hot water
½	cup grated Parmesan or Asiago cheese

To prepare artichokes, see recipe for Marinated Artichoke Hearts, Chapter 2. Before placing in bowl with lemon juice, cut each artichoke into 4 wedges and each wedge into ¼-inch-thick slices, lengthwise, and dice.

Place chopped parsley, garlic, and ham in a bowl and mix together. Heat oil in a saucepan, add ham mixture and sauté for 3 minutes. Add diced artichokes, sprinkle with pepper, lower heat, and cook uncovered for 10 minutes. Remove from heat and set aside.

In another saucepan, melt 2 tablespoons butter. Add sliced onion and cook for 2 minutes. Add rice and stir until well coated. Add artichoke mixture and 1 cup of hot broth and water; stir and cook gently. Continue adding broth and water before it is all absorbed and cook until rice is tender-firm, about 15 to 20 minutes. Remove from heat, stir in remaining 2 tablespoons of butter and the Parmesan cheese. Serve immediately. Serves 6.

RICE WITH ASPARAGUS
Risotto con asparagi

Tasty with any chicken dish.

1½	pounds fresh asparagus, or
10	ounces frozen or canned asparagus spears, defrosted
4	tablespoons sweet butter or margarine
1	small onion, thinly sliced
1½	cups Arborio Italian or long-grain rice
2	cups homemade or canned chicken broth
2	cups hot water
½	cup grated Parmesan or Asiago cheese

To prepare fresh asparagus, see directions in recipe for Asparagus and Prosciutto Rolls, Chapter 2.

In another saucepan melt butter. Add sliced onion and cook for 2 minutes. Add rice and stir until well coated. Add cut asparagus and 1 cup of broth and water. Stir-cook gently. Continue adding broth and water until it is all absorbed and continue cooking covered until rice is tender-firm, about 15 to 20 minutes. Remove from heat, stir in grated cheese. Serve immediately. Serves 6.

RICE WITH CARROTS AND PEAS

Risotto con carote e piselli

Preheat oven to 325°F.

- 4 tablespoons corn oil
- 1 small onion, sliced
- 10 ounces frozen diced carrots, defrosted, drained
- 10 ounces frozen peas, defrosted, drained
- 1½ cups Arborio Italian or long-grain rice
- 8 ounces canned plum tomatoes, drained and chopped
- 1 teaspoon dried basil
- 3 cups homemade or canned chicken broth
- ½ cup grated Parmesan or Asiago cheese
- 4 tablespoons sweet butter or margarine

In a skillet heat oil. Add onion and cook for 5 minutes. Add carrots and peas. Stir in rice and cook for 5 minutes. Transfer to a bake-and-serve casserole. Add tomatoes, basil, and broth; stir to mix. Top with grated cheese, dot with butter. Cover.

Bake for 45 minutes to 1 hour or until all the liquid has been absorbed. Serves 6.

CAULIFLOWER AND RICE CASSEROLE

Cavolfiore e riso al forno

Preheat oven to 400°F.

- 1 cauliflower, about 1½ pounds, chopped; reserve a few flowerets; or
- 2 10-ounce packages frozen cauliflower, thawed
- 2 cups homemade or canned chicken broth
- 2 cups water
- 1 cup Arborio Italian or long-grain rice
- 5 tablespoons melted butter or margarine
- ½ cup grated Parmesan cheese
- ¼ teaspoon white pepper
  pinch nutmeg
- 3 tablespoons unflavored bread crumbs
  parsley sprigs

Steam chopped cauliflower; drain well. In a saucepan, combine chicken broth and water. Bring to a boil. Add rice and simmer for 5 minutes. Drain.

In a bowl, combine cauliflower, rice, 3 tablespoons butter,

cheese, pepper, and nutmeg. Mix well. Transfer to a well-buttered bake-and-serve casserole. Mix 2 tablespoons melted butter with bread crumbs; sprinkle over top of cauliflower-rice mixture. Garnish with reserved flowerets and parsley sprigs. Bake for 10 minutes. Serves 6 to 8.

EGGPLANT WITH RICE
Riso con melanzane

1 large eggplant, about 1½ pounds, diced
4 tablespoons corn oil
2 cloves garlic, minced
4 sprigs fresh parsley
½ teaspoon salt
¼ teaspoon white pepper
2 cups water
2 cups homemade or canned chicken broth
1½ cups Arborio Italian or long-grain rice
½ cup grated Parmesan or Asiago cheese

Peel and dice eggplant.

Heat oil in a skillet; add garlic and diced eggplant. Stir and cook over medium heat for 10 minutes. Add parsley; stir and cook 5 minutes longer. Stir in salt and pepper and set aside. Keep warm.

In a saucepan combine water and broth; bring to a boil. Add rice; reduce heat and simmer uncovered until rice is tender but firm, about 15 to 20 minutes. Drain if necessary and transfer to a warm serving bowl. Pour eggplant mixture over; stir and serve immediately. Serve cheese in a separate bowl. Serves 6.

KALE WITH RICE
Risotto con cavolo riccio

2 pounds fresh kale
4 tablespoons corn oil
1 small onion, sliced
1 celery stalk, chopped
½ teaspoon salt
¼ teaspoon white pepper
1½ cups Arborio Italian or long-grain rice
2 cups homemade or canned hot chicken broth
3 tablespoons sweet butter (optional)

Cut off and discard kale's tough outer leaves and stalks. Rinse well in cold water. Place in vegetable steamer with 1 inch salted water. Cover and steam for 5 minutes. Drain well and set aside.

In a large skillet heat oil; add onion and celery. Cover and cook over medium heat for 5 minutes or until onion is soft. Sprinkle with salt and pepper. Add rice; stir to coat well. Add hot broth; stir. Reduce heat, cover, and cook for 15 minutes, stirring occasionally. Add well-drained kale; stir, cover, and cook for 10 more minutes, or until rice is tender but firm. Transfer to a warm serving bowl; stir in butter and serve. Serves 6.

LEEKS WITH RICE ALLA PIEMONTESE

Riso con salsa di porri alla Piemontese

10	large leeks
6	tablespoons sweet butter or margarine
1/2	teaspoon salt
1/2	teaspoon white pepper
1/2	cup dry white wine
2	cups homemade or canned chicken broth
2	cups water
1½	cups Arborio Italian or long-grain rice
1/2	cup grated Parmesan or Asiago cheese

To prepare leeks see directions in recipe for Leeks with Caper Sauce, Chapter 2.

Melt butter in a skillet. Add leeks and sauté over medium high heat for 10 minutes. Reduce heat to very low; cover and cook for 30 minutes.

After 15 minutes begin preparing rice. In a saucepan combine broth and water; bring to a boil; add rice. Reduce the heat and simmer uncovered until rice is tender but firm, about 12 to 14 minutes. Drain if necessary and transfer to a warm serving bowl. After 30 minutes sprinkle leek sauce with salt and pepper; add wine. Raise heat and cook and stir until the wine has evaporated. Taste for additional salt and pepper.

Pour leek sauce over rice in bowl. Top with grated cheese and serve immediately. Serves 6.

RICE AND PEAS
Riso con piselli

In the Venetian dialect, this dish is known as *risi e bisi*.

- 6 tablespoons sweet butter or margarine
- 4 ounces Italian prosciutto, thinly sliced, diced
- 1 medium onion, chopped
- 3 pounds fresh peas, shelled, or
- 20 ounces frozen peas, thawed
- 6 cups homemade or canned chicken broth
- 1½ cups Arborio Italian or long-grain rice
- 3 tablespoons chopped fresh parsley
- ½ cup grated Parmesan or Asiago cheese

In a large skillet melt 4 tablespoons butter. Add prosciutto and onions and sauté until onion is soft. Add peas; stir. Add broth. Cover and cook over low heat for 10 minutes.

Add rice and stir gently so as not to crush peas. Continue cooking over low heat, uncovered, for 15 to 20 minutes, or until rice is tender-firm and most of the liquid has evaporated. Stir in remaining butter with parsley. Remove from heat. Stir in grated cheese. Taste for additional salt and serve hot. Serves 6.

RICE WITH PEPPERS
Risotto con peperoni

- 4 tablespoons corn oil
- 1 medium onion, thinly sliced
- 1 celery stalk, chopped
- 2 medium green peppers and 2 medium red peppers, diced, or
- 4 green peppers, diced
- 8 ounces canned plum tomatoes, drained and chopped
- 4 leaves fresh basil, or
- ½ teaspoon dried basil
- ½ teaspoon salt
- ¼ teaspoon black pepper
- 1½ cups Arborio Italian or long-grain rice
- 2 cups homemade or canned chicken broth, hot
- 4 tablespoons sweet butter or margarine

In a large skillet, heat oil. Add onion, celery, and all peppers. Cover and cook over medium heat for 25 minutes. Stir in tomatoes, basil, salt, pepper, rice, and hot broth. Cover and cook over low heat for 30 minutes, stirring occasionally. Add a little hot water if needed. When rice is tender-firm, transfer to a warm serving bowl; stir in butter and serve immediately. Serves 6.

SPINACH RISOTTO
Risotto con spinaci

1	pound fresh spinach, steamed, drained and chopped, or
10	ounces frozen chopped spinach, thawed and drained
4	tablespoons corn oil
1	small onion, chopped
¼	teaspoon salt
¼	teaspoon black pepper
1½	cups Arborio Italian or long-grain rice
2	cups homemade or canned chicken broth, hot
4	tablespoons sweet butter or margarine
½	cup grated Parmesan or Asiago cheese

Prepare spinach, as indicated in above ingredients. Heat oil in a saucepan. Add onions, sprinkled with salt and pepper and cook until soft. Add rice and stir until well coated. Add spinach, and stir. Add 1 cup hot broth; stir and cook gently. Continue adding broth until it is all absorbed and cook covered until rice is tender but firm. Remove from heat. Stir in butter and cheese. Transfer to a warm serving bowl and serve. Serves 6.

RICE WITH FRESH TOMATOES
Riso con pomodori freschi

3	tablespoons sweet butter
1½	cups Arborio Italian or long-grain rice
1	pound sun-ripened tomatoes, or
1	16-ounce can chopped plum tomatoes, with their juice
1½	cups water
1½	teaspoons salt
2	teaspoons sugar
¼	teaspoon white pepper

In saucepan, melt butter. Add rice and stir until coated. If using fresh tomatoes, add 1½ cups of water; if using canned tomatoes, measure liquid from can and add enough water to equal 2 cups. Add liquid, tomatoes, salt, sugar, and pepper to rice. Cover and cook over low heat for 15 to 20 minutes, until the rice is tender-firm. Transfer to a warm serving bowl and serve immediately. Serves 6.

ZUCCHINI WITH RICE
Zucchine con riso

6	fresh zucchini, about 7 to 8 inches long
6	tablespoons sweet butter or margarine
½	teaspoon salt
¼	teaspoon white pepper
1½	cups Arborio Italian or long-grain rice
2	cups homemade or canned chicken broth
2	cups water
½	cup grated Parmesan or Asiago cheese

Wash zucchini; cut off both ends and discard. Cut crosswise into ¼-inch-thick slices.

Melt 3 tablespoons butter in skillet. Add zucchini and sauté for 10 minutes over medium heat. Sprinkle with salt and pepper. Remove from heat and keep warm.

Meanwhile, in a saucepan combine broth with water and bring to a boil. Add rice; stir; reduce heat and simmer, covered, for 10 to 12 minutes, or until rice is tender but firm. Drain rice if necessary and place in warm serving bowl. Top rice with sautéed zucchini. Add remaining butter to zucchini and rice and cheese and toss gently. Serve hot. Serves 6.

PASTA

**LASAGNE WITH
ARTICHOKES**

Lasagne con carciofi

Preheat oven to 375°F.

2 cups Béchamel sauce (see recipe in Chapter 5, Sauces)
6 medium artichokes
1 lemon
5 tablespoons sweet butter or margarine
½ cup water
   pinch salt
8 ounces thin lasagne
1 pound Ricotta cheese or skim milk cottage cheese
2 eggs
¾ cup grated Parmesan, or Asiago cheese

Prepare Béchamel sauce.

To prepare artichokes see recipe for Marinated Artichoke Hearts, Chapter 2. Before placing in bowl with lemon juice cut each artichoke into 8 wedges and cut each wedge into ¼-inch-thick slices, lengthwise.

Drain artichokes and transfer to a large skillet. Add 2 tablespoons butter, ½ cup water, and a pinch of salt. Cover and simmer for 15 minutes.

Cook lasagna according to package directions; set on towels to drain.

In a bowl combine Ricotta with eggs, and beat with electric beater for 5 minutes. (If by hand, beat until well blended.) Stir in Béchamel sauce.

Place one layer of cooked lasagne on bottom of buttered bake-and-serve lasagne pan. Over the lasagne spread a thin layer of Ricotta/Béchamel mixture, then a thin layer of artichokes; sprinkle with Parmesan cheese. Repeat until all the ingredients have been used, ending with lasagne topped with Béchamel sprinkled with Parmesan cheese. Dot with the remaining butter. Bake for 25 minutes. After removing pan from oven, allow lasagne to stand 10 minutes before serving. Serves 6 to 8.

ASPARAGUS BAKED WITH EGG NOODLES
Asparagi in forno con maltagliati

Maltagliati means "badly cut," and these noodles are square or rectangular, about one and one-half by two inches. I find the Bott Boi brand best.

Preheat oven to 350°F.

2	pounds fresh asparagus, or
20	ounces frozen or canned asparagus spears, defrosted, well drained
7	tablespoons sweet butter or margarine
1	small onion, finely chopped
1	pound maltagliati egg noodles
8	ounces Ricotta cheese or skim milk cottage cheese
2	eggs
½	teaspoon salt
¼	teaspoon white pepper
½	cup grated Parmesan or Asiago cheese

To prepare fresh asparagus see directions in recipe for Asparagus and Prosciutto Rolls, Chapter 2.

Melt 3 tablespoons butter in a skillet; add asparagus with chopped onion, cook over low heat until soft; if necessary add 2 or 3 tablespoons hot water.

In the meantime, cook noodles according to package directions; drain well, and add 3 tablespoons butter; toss gently to coat well.

Place half of cooked noodles on bottom of buttered bake-and-serve casserole. Over the noodles spread Ricotta cheese, then the asparagus pieces, and again, the remaining noodles. Beat the eggs with salt, pepper, and grated cheese. Pour over noodles. Bake for 15 minutes. Serve hot. Serves 6.

SPAGHETTI WITH GREEN BEANS AND EGGS
Spaghetti con fagiolini e uove

1	pound fresh green beans, or
10	ounces frozen cut green beans, defrosted
1	pound thin spaghetti
3	tablespoons sweet butter
½	cup grated Parmesan or Asiago cheese
	salt
	black pepper
3	eggs, well beaten

To prepare fresh beans, remove ends and strings from beans. Cut into 1-inch pieces. Place in vegetable steamer with 1 inch salted water. Cover and steam for 10 minutes. Drain well and keep warm. Cook frozen beans according to package directions; drain well, and keep warm.

Cook spaghetti according to package directions or to your liking; drain and return to saucepan, over very low heat. Add butter, cheese, salt, and pepper to taste, toss well. Add warm beans and remove from heat; add eggs, one at a time, stirring constantly until spaghetti is well coated. Serve immediately. Serves 6 to 8.

BROCCOLI WITH PASTA

Fettuccine con broccoli

1	large bunch of fresh broccoli, about 2 pounds, or
20	ounces frozen chopped broccoli, defrosted and drained
4	tablespoons olive oil
3	tablespoons sweet butter
2	cloves garlic, minced
½	teaspoon salt
½	teaspoon black pepper
1	pound fettuccine or any pasta of your choice
1	cup grated Pecorino or sharp cheddar cheese

To prepare broccoli, discard outer leaves. Cut off lower parts of stalks. Wash and place in a large saucepan; cover with salted water. Bring to a boil, lower heat, cover, and cook for 15 minutes. Drain and dice. Reserve water. (If using frozen broccoli, cook according to box directions.)

Heat oil and butter in a skillet, add drained broccoli, garlic, salt, and pepper, and cook over medium heat for 10 minutes, stirring occasionally. Remove from heat but keep warm.

Add enough water to the reserved water from broccoli to make about 8 cups; taste for additional salt. Bring to a boil and cook fettuccine according to package directions, or to your liking. Drain. Transfer to a warm serving bowl, top with cooked broccoli. Sprinkle with ½ cup grated cheese. Serve remaining cheese in a separate bowl. Serves 6.

EGG NOODLES WITH CARROTS
Tagliatelle con carote

1   pound fresh carrots, or
10 ounces frozen diced carrots, defrosted
4   tablespoons sweet butter or margarine
½ teaspoon crushed rosemary leaves
1   pound egg noodles
8   ounces baked ham, cut into long strips (julienne)
½ cup grated Parmesan or Asiago cheese

Scrape carrots; dice, wash, and drain.

Melt butter in skillet, add rosemary and carrots, stir. Cover and cook over medium heat for 10 minutes.

In the meantime, cook noodles according to package directions, drain, and transfer to a warm serving bowl. Add ham to carrots; stir to warm up. Pour carrot and ham mixture over cooked noodles; sprinkle with grated cheese. Toss gently and serve hot. Serves 4 to 6.

CAULIFLOWER WITH ZITI
Pasta con cavolfiore

Normally, according to the Italian method, cauliflower and pasta are cooked in the same water. I am a strong believer, however, in not pouring vitamins down the drain, so I prefer to steam the cauliflower. The result is as good as, if not better than, the Italian method.

1   cauliflower head, about 1½ pounds
6   tablespoons olive oil
3   large cloves garlic, minced
½ teaspoon black pepper
   salt to taste
1   pound thin spaghetti or fettucine
½ cup grated Parmesan or Asiago cheese

To prepare cauliflower, see directions in recipe for Cauliflower with Bagna Caôda, Chapter 2.

Heat oil in a skillet; add garlic and sauté until light gold.

Dice cauliflower and add to garlic in skillet. Sprinkle with pepper and sauté until cauliflower is tender. In the meantime, cook pasta according to package directions or to your liking; drain and place in a warm serving bowl. Add cauliflower, toss well, and sprinkle with grated cheese. Toss and serve hot. Serves 6.

KALE WITH NOODLES

Cavolo riccio con fettucine

Fast to make; good to eat.

1½ pounds fresh kale
 4 tablespoons sweet butter or margarine
 1 medium onion, chopped
 1 clove garlic, peeled
 3 anchovy fillets, chopped
 ½ teaspoon black pepper
 8 ounces egg noodles, broken into 1-inch pieces

Cut off and discard tough outer leaves and stalks from kale. Rinse well. Drain and cut into thin strips.

Melt butter in a skillet. Add onion and garlic and cook over medium heat until onion is soft. Discard garlic. Add chopped anchovies and pepper. Add shredded kale; stir. Reduce heat, cover, and cook for 30 minutes, stirring occasionally.

In the meantime, cook noodles in salted boiling water for 3 minutes. Drain. When kale is ready, add noodles, stir, and cook long enough for noodles to get hot. Serves 6.

MUSHROOMS AND MACARONI CASSEROLE

Maccheroni al forno con funghi

Preheat oven to 375°F.

 1 pound fresh mushrooms
 2 cups Béchamel sauce (see recipe in Chapter 5, Sauces)
 1 pound macaroni, ziti, or penne
 5 tablespoons sweet butter or margarine
 6 ounces Italian prosciutto, julienne
 1 small white truffle (optional)
 ½ teaspoon white pepper
 ⅛ teaspoon nutmeg
    salt to taste
 1 cup grated Parmesan or Asiago cheese

Wash mushrooms and slice thin; set aside.

Make Béchamel sauce.

Cook macaroni according to package directions; drain.

Melt 4 tablespoons butter in a skillet; add prosciutto, truffle, and mushrooms; sauté for 3 minutes. Remove from heat. Add half of the sauce to mushrooms; sprinkle with pepper and nutmeg; stir and taste for salt.

Butter a bake-and-serve dish well. Place macaroni in layers alternating with mushrooms and sauce mixture, sprinkling grated cheese over each layer. Finish with the remaining sauce and sprinkle with cheese. Bake for 25 minutes. Serves 6.

EGG NOODLES WITH PEAS
Tagliatelle con piselli

3	tablespoons olive oil
2	medium onions, finely chopped
4	ounces thinly sliced Italian prosciutto, julienne
2	pounds fresh peas, or
20	ounces frozen peas, thawed, drained
2	tablespoons chopped fresh parsley
1	teaspoon salt
¼	teaspoon white pepper
1	cup homemade or canned chicken broth
1	pound egg noodles
½	cup grated Parmesan or Asiago cheese

Heat oil in a skillet. Add onions and prosciutto; sauté over medium heat until onions are soft. Add peas, parsley, salt, and pepper and cook for 5 minutes, stirring occasionally. Add broth, cover skillet, and simmer over low heat for 20 minutes.

In the meantime, cook noodles according to package directions. Drain. Transfer to a warm serving bowl; pour sauce over; toss. Add grated cheese and toss again. Serve hot. Serves 6.

ZUCCHINI WITH PASTA
Zucchine con pasta

Any tubular kind of macaroni may be used.

8 fresh zucchini, about 7 to 8 inches long
1 large onion, thinly sliced
½ teaspoon salt
½ teaspoon white pepper
6 tablespoons sweet butter or margarine
1 pound macaroni of your choice (medium-size shells, wheels, corkscrews work well)
½ cup grated Parmesan or Asiago cheese

Wash zucchini; cut off both ends and discard. Cut zucchini crosswise into ¼-inch-thick slices.

Melt 5 tablespoons butter in skillet. Sauté onions until soft. Sprinkle with salt and pepper. Add sliced zucchini; sauté for 10 minutes, stirring occasionally. Remove from heat and keep warm.

Cook macaroni according to package directions, or to your taste. Drain and transfer to a warm serving bowl. Pour zucchini over; add remaining butter and grated cheese; toss gently. Serve hot. Serves 6.

DUMPLINGS
Gnocchi

POTATO DUMPLINGS ALLA PIEMONTESE
Gnocchi di patate alla Piemontese

2 pounds baking potatoes
2 egg yolks
2 tablespoons olive oil
½ teaspoon nutmeg
1 to 1½ cups flour
6 tablespoons sweet butter or margarine
½ cup grated Parmesan or Asiago cheese

Cook unpeeled potatoes in boiling salted water for 30 minutes, or until fork tender. Drain and peel as soon as they are cool enough to handle. Put them through a potato ricer or food processor and puree.

Transfer puree to a pastry board. Add egg yolks, oil, and nutmeg. Mix in flour, a little at a time, and knead into a smooth soft dough. Roll into a sausage-shaped long roll, about the thickness of your finger. Cut into 1-inch pieces.

Hold a piece of dough between two fingers. Hold fork in other hand. Take piece of dough and, starting at top of the tines, press it down toward cradle, making a deep depression in one side with thumb and ridges in other side.

Cook dumplings in several batches, about 20 in a pot at a time. Drop dumplings one by one into gently boiling salted water and cook for 5 to 7 minutes. Lift them out with a slotted spoon as they rise to the surface. Transfer to a warm serving bowl and dribble melted butter over them. When all are cooked, toss them very gently with the cheese, or omit butter and cheese and serve with Italian Meat Sauce (see recipe in Chapter 5, Sauces). Serves 6.

SPINACH DUMPLINGS
Gnocchi di spinaci

This recipe can also be a main dish when served with salad and dessert.

Preheat oven to 400°F.

3	pounds fresh spinach, or
30	ounces frozen chopped spinach, thawed
6	cups milk
1	cup semolina, or cream of wheat (farina)
4	tablespoons sweet butter or margarine
¼	teaspoon salt
¼	teaspoon white pepper
¼	teaspoon nutmeg
1½	cups grated Parmesan or Asiago cheese
1	egg
2	egg yolks
2	cups Béchamel sauce (see recipe in Chapter 5, Sauces)

Prepare fresh spinach by removing roots and hard stems. Wash in several changes of water.

Place spinach in vegetable steamer with 1 inch salted water. Cover and steam for 5 minutes. Drain and transfer to a blender or food processor and puree. Set aside.

In a saucepan heat 4 cups of the milk to boiling point. Lower the heat and add cream of wheat a little at a time, stirring constantly with a wooden spoon, until all has been added. Continue stirring and cook over very low heat for 10 minutes longer. Remove from heat and add 2 tablespoons butter, salt, pepper, and nutmeg; stir to mix. Add ½ cup grated cheese, the egg and the 2 yolks; stir in pureed spinach.

Make Béchamel sauce. When ready, remove from heat and stir in ½ cup grated cheese.

Butter a bake-and-serve dish well. Make little balls with teaspoonsful of spinach mixture and arrange them in a baking dish. Pour Béchamel sauce over; sprinkle with remaining grated cheese, and dot with the remaining butter. Bake for 20 minutes. Serves 6.

5

Sauces

Salse

NOTE: Most sauces, except for the Béchamel, can be frozen successfully for one week or, at the most, two weeks.

BASIL SAUCE (PESTO)
Pesto

Pesto is the name of a marvelous sauce made only with fresh basil. It can be stored in your freezer for up to one year.

3 cups fresh basil leaves
3 cloves garlic
½ teaspoon salt
½ teaspoon black pepper
½ cup olive oil
4 tablespoons *pinoli* (pine nuts)
4 tablespoons sweet butter

Remove all stems from basil (save for a soup). Wash the leaves and drain well. Place leaves in container of blender or food processor; add garlic, salt, pepper, and oil and process until coarsely chopped. It should *not* be creamy or mushy.

Transfer to a bowl; stir in pinoli.

Add butter to the warm vegetables, pasta, rice, or dumplings with which you are using this sauce.

This sauce freezes very well. To freeze, do not add nuts or butter; you will add them when you thaw and use the sauce. Makes enough to serve 6.

BÉCHAMEL SAUCE

Salsa Besciamella

The basic version of an all-purpose sauce that has many variations.

    4   tablespoons butter
    1   small onion, quartered (optional)
    4   tablespoons flour
    2   cups milk
    ½   teaspoon salt
    ¼   teaspoon white pepper
    ⅛   teaspoon nutmeg

In a small saucepan over low heat, melt butter. Add onion and sauté for a few minutes. Discard onion; add flour, stirring constantly until blended.

Meanwhile, scald milk in another saucepan. Pour all at once into butter-flour mixture and stir until thickened. Stir in salt, pepper, and nutmeg. Simmer slowly, stirring constantly for 10 minutes, until sauce is ready. Makes 2 cups.

EGGPLANT SAUCE FOR PASTA

Salsa di melanzane per pasta

A delicious way to prepare any type of pasta without meat.

    6   tablespoons corn oil
    1   medium onion, finely chopped
    1   clove garlic, minced
    1   medium eggplant, about 1 pound, peeled and diced
    1   green pepper, seeded, diced
    1   16-ounce can plum tomatoes, drained
    1   tablespoon chopped fresh basil, or
    1   teaspoon dried basil leaves
    ½   teaspoon marjoram
    ½   teaspoon black pepper
    ½   cup black olives, pitted
    6   anchovy fillets
    1   tablespoon capers
    1   pound thin spaghetti
    ½   cup grated Parmesan or Asiago cheese

Heat oil in a large skillet over medium heat. Add onion and garlic and sauté until soft. Add diced eggplant and green pepper and cook for 5 minutes, stirring frequently.

Place tomatoes, basil, marjoram, pepper, olives, anchovies, and capers in container of an electric blender or food processor. Process until coarsely chopped. Add to onion in skillet; stir. Cover and cook over low heat for 1 hour.

In the last 15 minutes of cooking time, bring a large saucepan of salted water to a boil and cook spaghetti according to directions on package, or to your liking. Drain spaghetti and place in warm serving bowl. Pour sauce over top; toss and serve. Serve cheese in separate bowl. Serves 6.

FENNEL SAUCE
Salsa di finocchi

Equally good with any pasta or boiled rice.

2	medium fennels
4	tablespoons olive oil
1	large onion, finely chopped
2	cloves garlic, minced
6	anchovy fillets, chopped
1	16-ounce can chopped plum tomatoes, with its juice
½	teaspoon oregano
1	teaspoon black pepper
	spaghetti or rice
2	tablespoons *pinoli* (pine nuts)

Remove tops and tough outer leaves of fennels and discard. Dice and rinse well. Drain and set aside.

Heat oil in a saucepan. Add onion and garlic and sauté until soft. Add chopped anchovies, chopped tomatoes with their juice, and oregano. Stir and cook over low heat for 10 minutes. Add diced fennels and ½ teaspoon pepper, stirring to mix. Cover and cook over very low heat for 1 hour, stirring occasionally.

At serving time, cook spaghetti or rice according to package instructions, or to your liking. Place spaghetti in warm serving bowl, and pour sauce over. Sprinkle with the pine nuts and pepper, toss, and serve hot. Serves 6.

GREEN MAYONNAISE

Salsa maionese verde

A variation of mayonnaise sauce that can be used with cold, steamed, or raw vegetables.

2 cups mayonnaise, (see recipe later in this chapter)
1 medium onion, finely chopped
2 tablespoons chopped fresh parsley
2 tablespoons chopped fresh tarragon
1½ teaspoons chopped capers
3 anchovy fillets

Place mayonnaise in container of a blender or food processor. Add onion, parsley, tarragon, capers, and anchovies. Cover and process until well blended and smooth. Makes 2½ cups.

FRESH TOMATO SAUCE FOR PASTA

Salsa di pomodori freschi per pasta

4 tablespoons olive oil
2 tablespoons sweet butter
2 medium onions, chopped
1 stalk celery, chopped
1 small carrot, chopped
2 cloves garlic
5 pounds fresh ripe tomatoes, peeled, chopped; or
3 16-ounce cans of plum tomatoes
8 fresh basil leaves, chopped
2 teaspoons salt
1 teaspoon white pepper

Heat oil in a saucepan; add butter, onions, celery, carrots, and garlic; cook over low heat until onion is soft and golden. Remove garlic and discard. Add tomatoes, basil, salt, and pepper. Simmer uncovered for 1½ hours.

Transfer tomatoes and all vegetables to the container of an electric blender or food processor; process until well pureed; or puree through a food mill. If using right away, return to saucepan to warm. If using canned plum tomatoes, simmer only for 45 minutes. Makes 4 to 5 cups.

GREEN SAUCE FOR ARTICHOKES
Salsa verde per carciofi

This sauce may be used with any vegetable, raw or cooked, but it is especially good with artichokes.

½ cup olive oil
1 large clove garlic
1 cup fresh basil leaves
3 tablespoons *pinoli* (pine nuts)
½ teaspoon salt
¼ teaspoon white pepper

Place all ingredients in the container of an electric blender or food processor. Cover and blend for a few seconds. Taste for additional salt and pepper. Serve with raw or cooked artichokes. Makes about 1 cup.

HOT ANCHOVY-GARLIC DIP
Bagna caôda

There is an old story that *bagna caôda* originated as a farmer's lunch during the grape harvest in the hilltops of Piemonte. It could be cooked at home, in an earthenware casserole, then brought to the vineyard where it was kept bubbling hot over an open fire. At noon, the men would sit around it, dipping a variety of raw vegetables into the sauce, and eating from a loaf of crusty Italian bread.

1 cup olive oil
½ cup butter
2 2-ounce cans anchovy fillets
12 cloves garlic, sliced very thin
1 small truffle (optional)
¼ cup heavy cream (optional)
    raw vegetables: celery, Savoy cabbage, cauliflower, spinach, peppers, zucchini, and any others you may like

Cut or tear vegetables into bite-size pieces.
    Put all ingredients, except vegetables, in an earthenware casserole and simmer very slowly for 1 hour. At the table put casserole over a burner with a very low flame. Each person dips

a selection of raw vegetables into the sauce. Serve with crusty Italian bread. Serves 6 to 8.

HOT TOMATO SAUCE FOR FISH
Salsa piccante di pomodori per pesce

6 fresh ripe tomatoes, peeled, seeded
1 small onion
½ celery stalk
1 teaspoon dry mustard
1 teaspoon white pepper
1 teaspoon pure grated horseradish
1 teaspoon wine vinegar
4 tablespoons olive oil
2 anchovy fillets
  salt

Place all the ingredients in the container of an electric blender or food processor; process until finely chopped. Taste for additional salt and vinegar. Spread over poached or boiled fish. Chill before serving. Serves 6.

BOLOGNESE SAUCE (ITALIAN MEAT SAUCE)
Salsa di pomodori alla Bolognese

4 tablespoons olive oil
1 clove garlic
6 slices bacon, chopped
1 medium onion, chopped
1 large carrot, chopped
8 ounces sweet Italian sausages, chopped
8 ounces lean chopped beef
  salt and pepper to taste
½ cup dry white wine
8 ounces peeled plum tomatoes, chopped

Sauté garlic clove whole in oil for a few minutes; discard. Add bacon to oil, sauté for 5 minutes, and stir in chopped onion and carrot. Cook over low heat until onion is golden. Add sausage meat, cook, and stir for 10 minutes over high heat. Add chopped beef, salt, and pepper, and cook, stirring, until meat has browned. Add wine; cook for a few minutes longer. Lower the heat and add tomatoes. Cover and simmer for 1½ hours. Uncover and cook 30 minutes longer or until sauce has thickened. Serves 6.

MAYONNAISE
Salsa maionese

All ingredients should be at room temperature. If the mayonnaise *impazzisce* (goes crazy), that is, if the oil and eggs separate, it is very easy to save it. Begin again, using 1 egg yolk, and instead of new oil, add very slowly the "crazy" mayonnaise, beating constantly. You can also make mayonnaise using the food processor.

3 egg yolks
3 cups olive or corn oil
  juice of 3 lemons, strained
1 teaspoon salt
½ teaspoon white pepper

With a wire whisk, beat egg yolks in a bowl. Then, almost drop by drop, add oil very slowly, beating constantly. After incorporating all the oil, gradually add strained lemon juice, salt, and pepper. Makes 3 cups.

MIXED VEGETABLE SAUCE FOR PASTA OR RICE
Salsa di verdure per pasta o riso

1 pound fresh small asparagus, green parts only, cut diagonally into ½-inch pieces
8 ounces fresh broccoli, broken into small flowerets
8 ounces fresh cauliflower, broken into small flowerets
1 medium zucchini, cut into ¼-inch-thick round slices
2 small carrots, cut into ¼-inch-thick round slices
8 ounces fresh mushrooms, thinly sliced
1½ pounds *fettuccine*
10 tablespoons sweet butter or margarine
6 green onions, thinly sliced
4 shallots, chopped
1 tablespoon chopped fresh parsley
2 tablespoons chopped fresh basil
1 teaspoon salt
½ teaspoon white pepper
¼ teaspoon nutmeg
8 ounces shelled fresh peas
6 ounces cooked ham, julienne
1 cup grated Parmesan or Asiago cheese

Prepare all the vegetables and set aside.

Cook fettuccine according to directions on package, or to your liking; drain well; toss with 4 tablespoons of butter; return to saucepan, cover, and keep warm.

Melt remaining 6 tablespoons butter in a large skillet, add green onions and shallots; sauté for 3 minutes. Add asparagus, broccoli, cauliflower, zucchini, carrots, mushrooms, parsley, and basil; sprinkle with salt, pepper, and nutmeg, stir and cook over medium high heat for 5 minutes. Add peas and ham, and cook and stir for 3 minutes longer.

Transfer fettuccine to a warm large serving bowl; pour vegetable mixture over top; sprinkle with grated cheese and toss well. Serve immediately. Serves 6 to 8.

MUSHROOM SAUCE
Salsa di funghi

Equally good with egg noodles or boiled rice.

1   bunch fresh parsley
2   cloves garlic
1   teaspoon dried rosemary leaves
6   tablespoons sweet butter or margarine
2   pounds fresh firm mushrooms or Shiitake mushrooms
1   teaspoon salt
½   teaspoon white pepper

Remove all the stems from the parsley. Wash and drain. Place in container of a blender or food processor. Add garlic and rosemary and process until finely chopped.

Melt butter in a saucepan, add parsley mixture, and sauté for 5 minutes.

Wash and pat the mushrooms dry, cut into ¼-inch-thick slices and add to parsley in skillet. Sprinkle with salt and pepper and sauté, uncovered, for 10 minutes. Sauce is ready for use. Makes enough sauce for 1 pound of noodles or 2 cups of uncooked rice. Serve with plenty of grated Parmesan or Asiago cheese.

ONION SAUCE
Salsa di cipolle

Good with pasta, rice, or sliced hot or cold roast beef.

4 tablespoons sweet butter or margarine
3 tablespoons olive oil
4 cups chopped onions
3 cloves garlic, chopped
1 cup homemade or canned beef broth
1 cup dry white wine
2 whole cloves
3 bay leaves
1 teaspoon dried tarragon
½ teaspoon white pepper
   salt to taste

Melt butter in a saucepan with oil. Add onions and garlic and sauté over medium heat until onions are golden and soft. Add broth, wine, cloves, bay leaves, tarragon, and pepper. Bring to a boil, reduce heat, and cover and simmer for 30 minutes, stirring occasionally. Taste for salt. Transfer to container of a blender or food processor and puree. Reheat before serving. Makes about 2 cups.

PEPPER SAUCE
Salsa di peperoni

For spaghetti, or any kind of pasta, and boiled or steamed rice.

4 large green or red peppers
1 large onion, chopped
1 small clove garlic, minced
3 tablespoons olive oil
3 tablespoons sweet butter or margarine
1 cup homemade or canned chicken broth
½ teaspoon black pepper
   salt to taste
½ cup grated Parmesan or Asiago cheese
1 pound egg noodles, or
1½ cups long grain rice

Cut peppers in half lengthwise; remove seeds and pith; dice, rinse, and drain well.

Place peppers in a saucepan with onion, garlic, oil, and butter. Sauté over medium heat for 5 minutes. Add broth and pepper; stir. Reduce heat and simmer uncovered for 15 minutes. Taste for additional salt.

Transfer sauce to a blender or food processor and puree. Reheat before using. Stir in cheese and serve with cooked noodles or cooked rice. Serves 6.

RAW TOMATO SAUCE FOR SPAGHETTI

Salsa di pomodori crudi

2½ pounds fresh ripe tomatoes, peeled, and cut into ½-inch-thick slices
6 fresh basil leaves, finely chopped
4 fresh parsley sprigs, finely chopped
3 tablespoons fresh lemon juice
3 tablespoons olive oil
½ teaspoon salt
¼ teaspoon white pepper
1 pound thin spaghetti

In a large bowl combine tomatoes, basil, parsley, lemon juice, oil, salt, and pepper; toss gently and set aside.

Cook spaghetti according to package instructions, or to your liking; drain; transfer to a warm serving bowl. Pour tomato sauce over; toss gently and serve immediately. Serves 6.

SPINACH SAUCE FOR NOODLES

Salsa di spinaci per fettuccine

Terrific with homemade noodles.

1 pound fresh spinach, or
10 ounces frozen chopped spinach, thawed and drained
6 sprigs fresh parsley
2 cloves garlic
2 tablespoons *pinoli* (pine nuts)
4 tablespoons olive oil
1 teaspoon salt
½ teaspoon white pepper
grated Parmesan or Asiago cheese

Wash fresh spinach well; drain fresh or frozen spinach. Place in container of a blender or food processor. Add parsley, garlic, pine nuts and oil; puree. Transfer to a bowl; stir in salt and pepper, and your sauce is ready to use. Enough for 1 pound of egg noodles. Serve with plenty of grated cheese. Serves 6.

SWEET AND SOUR SAUCE
Salsa agrodolce

To be served over cooked vegetables.

¾ cup white wine vinegar
4 tablespoons sugar
4 egg yolks
½ cup water
¼ teaspoon salt
½ teaspoon white pepper
½ teaspoon prepared mustard (optional)

In a small saucepan combine vinegar and sugar. Beat in egg yolks one at a time. Add water, salt, pepper, and mustard; stir well. Heat over very low flame, stirring constantly. Cook until sauce is thickened and smooth; do not boil. Serve hot over steamed and drained vegetables. Makes about 1½ cups.

6 Main Dishes
Meat, Poultry, Fish

Carne, pollame, pesce

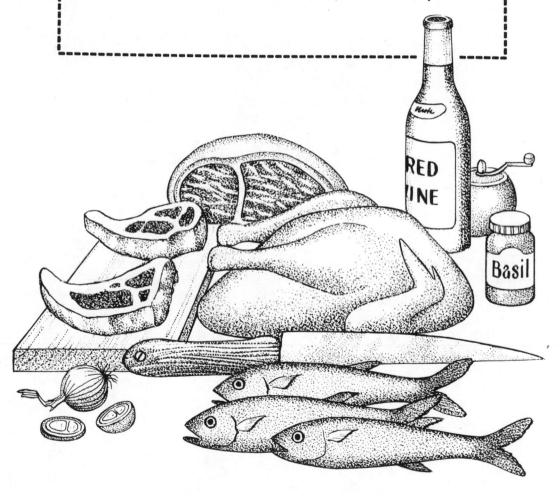

MEAT
Carne

ITALIAN GREEN BEANS WITH MEAT SAUCE

Taccole con sugo di carne

This dish can be used as a main dish, accompanied by soup and fruit.

For meat sauce:
- 1 medium onion
- 1 medium carrot
- 1 celery stalk
- 4 tablespoons olive oil
- 8 ounces lean round of beef, finely chopped
- 1 teaspoon salt
- ½ teaspoon black pepper
- ⅛ teaspoon nutmeg
- ½ cup dry white wine
- 1 16-ounce can chopped Italian plum tomatoes, with their juice
- 2 bay leaves
- ½ teaspoon rosemary leaves

For green beans:
- 20 ounces frozen Italian green beans
- ½ cup grated Parmesan or Asiago cheese

To prepare sauce, place onion, carrot, and celery in container of an electric blender or food processor and process until coarsely chopped. Heat oil in a saucepan, add onion mixture, and cook until onion is golden. Add chopped meat, salt, pepper, and nutmeg. Cook, stirring, until meat has browned. Add wine and continue stirring until wine has evaporated. Add chopped tomatoes and their juice, bay leaves, and rosemary leaves. Simmer slowly, uncovered, for 1 hour. Taste for additional salt and pepper.

Cook beans according to package directions. Drain well. Transfer to a warm shallow serving dish. Pour sauce over center of beans, sprinkle with grated cheese, and serve hot. Serves 6.

BEETS WITH MEAT SAUCE
Barbabietole con sugo di carne

Certainly less calories than spaghetti. . .

Preheat oven to 350°F.

2	pounds fresh beets, or
32	ounces canned sliced beets, drained
2	cups Italian Meat Sauce (see recipe in Chapter 5, Sauces)
½	cup grated Parmesan or Asiago cheese
	oil

Wash unpeeled beets. Place in vegetable steamer with 1 inch salted water and steam for 15 minutes. Drain, cool, and peel. Cut into ½-inch-thick round slices. Place beets in alternate layers with meat sauce in a well-oiled bake-and-serve dish, ending with sauce. Sprinkle with grated cheese. Bake for 20 minutes. Serves 6.

SAUTÉED ONIONS WITH LEFTOVER COOKED MEAT
Carne rifatta con cipolle

4	tablespoons corn oil
4	large onions, peeled and thinly sliced
1	clove garlic, mashed
2	cups diced boiled or roasted leftover meat, beef, or veal
1	beef bouillon cube, crumbled
½	cup homemade or canned beef broth
½	teaspoon white pepper

Heat oil in a skillet; add onions and garlic, and sauté over medium heat until onions are golden. Add meat, beef bouillon cube, broth, and pepper. Cover and simmer for 15 minutes. Uncover, raise the heat, and cook until all the liquid has evaporated. Taste for additional salt, and serve hot. Serves 6.

POTATO SAUTÉED WITH BEEF

Patate con carne frittata

7	medium potatoes
4	tablespoons sweet butter or margarine
1	pound lean chopped beef
2	cups milk
2	beef bouillon cubes, crumbled
1	teaspoon salt
½	teaspoon black pepper

Peel potatoes and cut into slices about ¼ inch thick. Wash and dry well.

Melt butter in a large saucepan. Add potatoes and sauté over medium heat until golden. Stir in meat, milk, beef bouillon cubes, salt, and pepper. Reduce heat, cover and simmer for 40 minutes, or until milk has been absorbed. Serve hot. Serves 6.

SPINACH AND MEAT LOAF

Polpettone di spinaci e carne

In this recipe, spinach acts as a meat stretcher. Those who claim not to like spinach will not even know that it is a main ingredient.

Preheat oven to 350°F.

2	pounds ground lean beef
1	pound fresh spinach, steamed and chopped, or
10	ounces frozen chopped spinach, thawed and drained
3	eggs, beaten
1½	teaspoons salt
½	teaspoon black pepper
2	tablespoons chopped fresh parsley
3	tablespoons wheat germ
	oil

In a large mixing bowl, combine meat, spinach, eggs, salt, pepper, and parsley. Mix well and form into an 8-inch loaf. Place in a greased 8 × 4-inch baking dish. Sprinkle with wheat germ.

Bake for 1 hour and 15 minutes. Serve sliced, with your favorite sauce or gravy. Serves 6.

VEAL STEW WITH SMALL ONIONS
Spezzatino di vitello con cipolline

Equally good with lean lamb cubes. Serve with boiled noodles or rice.

Preheat oven to 350°F.

2	tablespoons sweet butter or margarine
2	tablespoons corn oil
2	pounds trimmed boneless veal, cut into 1-inch cubes
2	small onions, quartered
1	clove garlic, chopped
2	tablespoons flour
1	teaspoon salt
½	teaspoon black pepper
1	cup homemade or canned beef broth
8	ounces canned plum tomatoes, chopped
½	teaspoon crumbled dried thyme
1	celery stalk with leaves plus 2 sprigs parsley, tied together
2	pounds small white onions, peeled
2	tablespoons chopped fresh parsley

Melt butter in a large skillet and add oil. Brown veal cubes on all sides. Add 2 small quartered onions, garlic, and flour. Cook, stirring, for 5 minutes. Add salt, pepper, broth, chopped tomatoes, thyme, and celery with parsley. Stir and transfer to a large casserole or baking pan; cover tightly.

Bake for 1 hour. Remove celery and parsley; add peeled small onions; cover and return to oven; cook 30 minutes longer. Before serving, stir in chopped parsley. Serves 6.

SCALOPPINE WITH PEAS

Scaloppine con piselli

Excellent with boiled rice and fruit for dessert.

1½ pounds veal *scaloppine* or beef tenderloin cut ¼ inch thick
½ teaspoon salt
1 cup flour
4 tablespoons sweet butter or margarine
4 tablespoons corn oil
2 pounds fresh peas, shelled, or
10 ounces frozen peas, thawed
½ cup dry Marsala wine
1 beef bouillon cube, crushed
½ cup hot water
1 tablespoon flour

Cut each *scaloppina* (singular of scaloppine) in half. Pound it flat between two pieces of waxed paper. Season with salt. Dip each scaloppina in flour on both sides; shake off any excess.

Over medium heat melt butter in a large skillet; add oil and sauté scaloppine, a few at a time, for 2 minutes on each side. Transfer to a warm serving dish and keep warm.

In the same skillet, with remaining fat, cook fresh peas for 10 minutes, or defrosted peas for 5 minutes. Add wine and bouillon dissolved in water; stir in flour; cook over high heat for 2 minutes. Return scaloppine to the skillet for 2 minutes to reheat. Add salt to taste. Serve hot. Serves 6.

SAUTÉED SCALOPPINE WITH TOMATO

Scaloppine con salsa di pomodoro

12 veal *scaloppine* or beef tenderloin, ¼ inch thick, about 2 to 2½ pounds
½ teaspoon salt
¼ teaspoon white pepper
1 cup flour
6 tablespoons butter
1 medium onion, finely chopped
1 8-ounce can chopped plum tomatoes, drained
3 fresh basil leaves
½ cup dry vermouth

Place each *scaloppina* between two pieces of waxed paper and pound thin. Cut slices in half. Season with salt and pepper. Dip in flour on both sides; shake off excess.

Melt butter in a large skillet over medium-high heat and sauté scaloppine 2 minutes on each side in several batches to prevent crowding. Transfer to a warm serving dish; cover and keep warm.

Add onion to remaining butter in skillet and sauté until golden. Add tomatoes and basil leaves; lower heat and cook for 10 minutes. Add vermouth and simmer 10 minutes longer. Remove basil leaves. Pour sauce over scaloppine and serve immediately. Serves 6.

PEAS WITH COTECHINO

Piselli in umido con cotechino

Cotechino, an Italian sausage, gets its name from *cotenna*, meaning pork rind, which is ground and mixed with the pork meat in the sausage. Look for it in Italian meat markets.

1	1-pound cotechino
4	tablespoons sweet butter or margarine
1	medium onion, finely chopped
1	clove garlic, minced
2	tablespoons flour
2	cups homemade or canned beef broth
4	sage leaves, or
1	teaspoon dried sage
2	pounds fresh peas, shelled, or
20	ounces frozen peas, thawed
½	teaspoon white pepper
	salt to taste

In a small kettle cover cotechino with cold water and soak for 1 hour. Prick cotechino with a fork; add more water to kettle and bring to a boil. Lower the heat; cover and simmer for 2 hours. Turn off heat. Peel and cut into ½-inch-thick slices; keep warm.

Melt butter in a large skillet. Add onion and garlic and sauté over medium heat until onion is soft, about 5 minutes. Stir in flour; add broth, sage leaves, and cotechino slices. Cook for 10 minutes. Add peas and sprinkle with pepper. Cover and cook over low heat for 20 more minutes. Taste for salt, and serve hot. Serves 6.

CARDOON WITH COTECHINO
Cardi con cotechino

Preheat oven to 350°F.

1 pound *cotechino*, cooked, peeled, diced
2½ pounds fresh cardoons
1 lemon
½ teaspoon salt
½ teaspoon white pepper
  oil
½ cup grated Parmesan or Asiago cheese
4 tablespoons sweet butter or margarine
3 tablespoons flour
1 cup milk
½ cup wheat germ

To prepare cotechino see preceding recipe, Peas with Cotechino. While cotechino is cooking, prepare cardoons.

Take the leaves off (they are very bitter). Cut each cardoon stalk into 2-inch pieces, removing any strings and skin as you cut, as you would with celery. Drop into a bowl of cold water to which the juice of 1 lemon has been added, to prevent cardoons from turning brown. Rinse and drain. Place in vegetable steamer over 1 inch salted water; cover and steam for 15 minutes. Drain and arrange cardoons in a well-oiled bake-and-serve shallow dish, in one layer.

Peel and dice cotechino and scatter over cardoons. Sprinkle with salt, pepper, and cheese. Stir flour into cold milk and pour over mixture. Dot with butter and sprinkle with wheat germ.

Bake for 15 minutes. Serve hot. Serves 6.

TURNIPS AND SAUSAGE LOAF

Polpettone di rape e salciccia

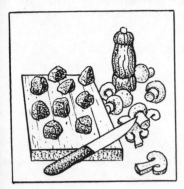

Preheat oven to 350°F.

- 2 pounds white turnips or rutabagas
- 1 pound sausage
- ½ cup chopped onion
- 1 cup chopped celery
- ½ cup chopped carrots
- 1 teaspoon salt
- ½ teaspoon white pepper
- 1 teaspoon tarragon
  oil

Peel turnips and cut into small cubes. Place in vegetable steamer over 1 inch salted water. Cover and steam for 10 minutes. Drain and transfer to a mixing bowl.

Remove skin from sausage and crumble the meat into a skillet. Cook over medium heat until sausage is lightly browned and all the fat has been rendered out. With a slotted spoon transfer sausage meat to mixing bowl with turnips. Add onion, celery, and carrots to the fat remaining in the skillet; cook until carrots are soft, about 10 minutes. Drain off fat and add vegetables to turnip-sausage mixture; sprinkle with salt, pepper, and tarragon. Mix well. Place mixture in a well-oiled loaf pan. Bake for 30 minutes. Serve hot. Serves 6.

LAMB STEW WITH MUSHROOMS

Fricando d'agnello con funghi

- 3 tablespoons sweet butter or margarine
- 3 tablespoons corn oil
- 3 pounds trimmed boneless lamb, cut into 1-inch cubes
- 1 clove garlic
- 3 bay leaves
- 1½ teaspoons salt
- ½ teaspoon black pepper
- 1 cup water
- ½ cup dry white wine
- 1 pound fresh mushrooms, sliced

Heat butter and oil in a Dutch oven and brown lamb cubes on all sides. Add garlic, bay leaves, salt, pepper, water, and wine. Cover, and cook over low heat for 2 hours. Remove garlic and bay leaves. Add mushrooms and cook uncovered for 15 minutes longer. Transfer to a warm serving dish. Serve with boiled rice. Serves 6.

POULTRY
Pollame

ARTICHOKE WITH CHICKEN
Carciofi con pollo

Egg noodles go well with this dish.

  2 large artichokes, or
20 ounces frozen or canned artichoke hearts
  1 lemon
  4 tablespoons sweet butter or margarine
  2 tablespoons corn oil
  1 3-pound frying chicken, cut into serving pieces
10 scallions, white parts only, sliced
½ teaspoon salt
¼ teaspoon white pepper
  4 bay leaves
  2 tablespoons lemon juice
½ cup dry white wine

To prepare fresh artichokes, see recipe for Marinated Artichoke Hearts, Chapter 2. Before placing in bowl with lemon juice, cut artichoke in 4 wedges and then cut wedges into ¼-inch-thick slices, lengthwise. If using frozen or canned artichoke hearts, defrost and drain well; cut each into 4 wedges, and add to chicken only for the last 5 minutes of cooking time.

In a large skillet heat the butter and oil. Add the chicken and brown on all sides. Remove and set aside.

In the same skillet sauté scallions and fresh artichokes, until artichokes are golden brown. Sprinkle with salt and pepper; add bay leaves and lemon juice. Return chicken to skillet, cover and cook over low heat for 30 minutes. Before serving, transfer chicken to a warm serving dish, and keep warm. Discard bay leaves. Loosen residue from bottom of skillet, add wine, return to high heat, stir and cook for 2 or 3 minutes, until sauce thickens. Pour over chicken and serve. Serves 6.

ASPARAGUS WITH CHICKEN
Asparagi con pollo

This recipe uses the stir-fry Chinese method, which is common in Italy.

1½	pounds chicken breasts, skinned and boned
¼	cup corn oil
2	teaspoons dried tarragon leaves
1	lemon
½	teaspoon salt
½	teaspoon white pepper
20	fresh asparagus spears

Cut chicken breasts into very thin strips. Place in a bowl with oil, tarragon, the juice from the lemon, salt, and pepper. Stir to mix well and set aside for 30 minutes at room temperature.

To prepare fresh asparagus, see recipe for Asparagus and Prosciutto Rolls, Chapter 2. Drain well and cut asparagus into 1-inch pieces.

Warm up a large heavy skillet or a wok. Add chicken mixture, including the oil. Cook and stir over high heat for 2 minutes. Remove chicken and add asparagus to juices in skillet, cooking and stirring for 2 minutes. Return chicken to skillet, and cook and stir for 1 minute. Serve hot with steamed or boiled rice. Serves 6.

GREEN OR WAX BEAN LOAF WITH CHICKEN
Polpettone di fagiolini con pollo

Preheat oven to 350°F.

1½ pounds fresh green or wax beans, or
10 ounces frozen cut green beans, defrosted and drained
3 slices stale whole-wheat bread
¼ cup milk
1 pound chicken or turkey breast, coarsely chopped
8 ounces Mortadella, coarsely chopped
3 eggs
¼ cup grated Parmesan or Asiago cheese
1 teaspoon salt
½ teaspoon white pepper
⅛ teaspoon nutmeg
2 tablespoons corn oil
¼ cup wheat germ

Remove ends and strings from fresh beans and cut into 1-inch pieces. Place in vegetable steamer with 1 inch of salted water. Cover and steam for 7 minutes. Drain.

Soak bread in milk; drain and squeeze out any excess.

In a large bowl combine beans, soaked bread, chopped chicken breast, Mortadella, eggs, grated cheese, salt, pepper, and nutmeg. Using your hands, mix well without breaking beans. Transfer to a well-oiled loaf pan and sprinkle top with wheat germ. Bake for 1 hour, or until an inserted knife comes out clean. Turn onto a warm serving dish and serve. Serve this loaf with your favorite mushroom sauce, if desired. Serves 6.

RED KIDNEY BEANS WITH TARRAGON CHICKEN

Fagioli borlotti con dragoncello e pollo

1½ cups dried red kidney beans
1 tablespoon chopped shallots
2 teaspoons dried tarragon leaves
4 whole peppercorns
¼ teaspoon salt
¼ cup tarragon vinegar
5 egg yolks
6 tablespoons sweet butter, melted
⅛ teaspoon white pepper
1 clove garlic, minced
2 tablespoons sweet butter or margarine
1 medium onion, thinly sliced
1½ cups diced cooked chicken or turkey

Wash dried beans thoroughly. Place in bowl, cover with water, and soak overnight. Or, boil beans for 3 minutes; remove from heat, cover pot, and let stand for 2 hours.

Drain beans. Place in a saucepan; cover with hot water plus 2 inches. Bring to a boil; reduce heat, cover saucepan, and simmer for 1½ hours, or until beans are tender.

To make sauce, place shallots, tarragon, peppercorns, salt, and vinegar in a small saucepan; simmer for 10 minutes. Remove from heat; cool. Add egg yolks, one at a time, beating with a wire whisk after each addition. Return to low heat; gradually add melted butter. Stir until sauce thickens. Add pepper, and taste for additional salt. Remove from heat.

Sauté garlic in 2 tablespoons butter for 2 minutes; discard garlic and add sliced onion to butter. Sauté until soft. Add beans and diced chicken. Stir over low heat for a few minutes.

Warm up sauce. Transfer bean-chicken mixture to a warm serving dish, pour sauce over, and serve. Serves 6.

CARROT AND CHICKEN STEW

Pollo in umido con carote

This is a good dish for a buffet. It may be prepared ahead of time and reheated. Freezes well.

1	4-pound stewing chicken, cut in pieces
3	tablespoons corn oil
3	tablespoons sweet butter
2	medium onions, thinly sliced
1	stalk celery, chopped
1½	pounds carrots, scraped and cut in ¼-inch slices
1	cup dry white wine
1	teaspoon salt
½	teaspoon black pepper
2	bay leaves
2	whole cloves
1	teaspoon dry thyme leaves
⅔	cup hot water or chicken broth

Wash chicken and pat dry with paper towels.

Heat oil and butter in a large skillet. Add chicken and brown well on all sides. Add onions, celery, and carrots. Cover and cook over low heat for 15 minutes. Add wine, salt, pepper, bay leaves, cloves, thyme, and ½ cup hot water or chicken broth. Cover and cook over low heat for 1 hour and 15 minutes.

As it cooks, turn chicken pieces occasionally. If necessary, add 2 or 3 tablespoons of hot water or broth, to prevent drying. Remove bay leaves and cloves. Transfer to a warm serving bowl and serve. Serve with rice. Serves 6 to 8.

CELERY, CARROT, AND CHICKEN STEW

Pollo in umido con sedani e carote

3	tablespoons corn oil
3	tablespoons sweet butter or margarine
4	pounds broiler-fryer chicken, cut into serving pieces
3	medium onions, thinly sliced
6	large carrots, cut into ¼-inch-thick rounds
6	celery stalks, with some leaves, diced
1	teaspoon salt
½	teaspoon white pepper
½	teaspoon tarragon

Heat oil in a large skillet; add butter and brown chicken pieces well on both sides. Transfer chicken to a warm serving dish and set aside.

To the oil remaining in skillet add the onions, carrots, celery, salt, pepper, and tarragon. Stir; cover and cook over medium-low heat for 15 minutes. Return chicken pieces to skillet with vegetables; cover and cook over low heat for 35 to 40 minutes, or until chicken is fork tender. Taste for additional salt and pepper and serve. Serves 6.

JERUSALEM ARTICHOKES WITH CHICKEN
Topinambur con pollo

3	pounds Jerusalem artichokes
1	lemon
6	tablespoons corn oil
2	whole chicken breasts, skinned, boned, and cut into 1-inch strips
10	ounces fresh or frozen peas, defrosted and well drained
4	tablespoons dry Marsala or port wine
½	teaspoon salt
½	teaspoon white pepper
1	tablespoon chopped fresh dill

To prepare Jerusalem artichokes, see recipe for Jerusalem Artichokes with Bagna Caôda, Chapter 2. Set aside bowl with artichokes soaking in lemon juice.

Heat oil in a large skillet; add chicken strips; cook and stir over medium-high heat for 2 minutes. Transfer chicken to a warm serving dish and set aside. Drain artichokes well, and pat dry between paper towels; add artichokes to oil remaining in skillet; cook and stir for 2 minutes. Drain off remaining oil from skillet and discard. Return chicken to skillet with artichokes; add well-drained peas, wine, salt, pepper, and dill. Stir and cook for 2 more minutes. Serve hot with mashed potatoes or boiled rice. Serves 6.

ROMAINE LETTUCE LEAVES STUFFED WITH CHICKEN

Foglie di lattuga ripiene di pollo

Preheat oven to 350°F.

6	tablespoons sweet butter or margarine
3	tablespoons corn oil
1	small onion, finely chopped
1	small clove garlic, minced
1	pound fresh mushrooms, thinly sliced
1	chicken bouillon cube, crumbled
4	tablespoons dry white wine
½	cup homemade or canned chicken broth
1	pound chicken breast, cooked and coarsely chopped
3	tablespoons wheat germ
2	eggs, slightly beaten
8	tablespoons grated Swiss cheese
¼	teaspoon white pepper
⅛	teaspoon nutmeg
	salt
20	leaves romaine lettuce
2	tablespoons chopped fresh parsley

Melt 3 tablespoons butter in a skillet; add 2 tablespoons oil; stir in onion and garlic; cook over medium heat for 5 minutes. Add mushrooms and bouillon cube; stir and cook 5 minutes longer. Add wine; raise the heat and cook until wine has evaporated. Add broth, stir, and cook 3 more minutes. Remove from heat; add chicken, wheat germ, eggs, 4 tablespoons grated cheese, pepper, nutmeg and parsley, mix well. Taste for additional salt, cover and refrigerate for 30 minutes.

In the meantime, remove ribs from lettuce leaves; place lettuce leaves in the basket of a vegetable steamer with 1 inch salted water. Cover and steam for 2 minutes. Drain well over paper towels. Try to cut the leaves into pieces of the same size, about 5 × 5 inches, so that you will have uniform rolls.

Place 2 tablespoons of chicken mixture onto each piece of lettuce, and close carefully by folding in the sides first, then the top. Arrange the lettuce rolls side by side, seam side down, in a well-buttered bake-and-serve dish. Melt remaining butter, brush over top of rolls; sprinkle with the remaining grated cheese. Bake, uncovered, for 15 minutes. Serve hot. Serves 6.

PEPPERS AND CHICKEN

Peperoni in padella con pollo

6	tablespoons corn oil
3	tablespoons sweet butter or margarine
2	large onions, thinly sliced
1	clove garlic, minced
½	teaspoon crumbled rosemary leaves
2	medium carrots, diced
1	celery stalk, diced
½	cup flour
12	chicken legs
6	red or green sweet peppers, seeded and cut into 1-inch strips
1	tablespoon tomato paste
½	cup dry white wine
1	chicken bouillon cube, crumbled
2	bay leaves
4	anchovy fillets, chopped
3	tablespoons wine vinegar
	salt
½	teaspoon white pepper
2	tablespoons chopped fresh parsley

Heat 3 tablespoons oil in a large skillet; add butter, onions, garlic, rosemary, carrots, and celery; cook over medium heat for 15 minutes, or until onions are golden.

Place flour in a plastic bag; shake chicken legs in it, a few at a time, to coat with flour.

Heat remaining 3 tablespoons oil in another skillet and brown chicken legs well. Transfer browned chicken legs to the skillet with onion and carrots; add peppers, and cook over medium-high heat for 10 minutes; shake skillet from time to time, to prevent scorching. Stir tomato paste into wine; add to chicken; add crumbled chicken bouillon cube, bay leaves, anchovies, vinegar, salt, and pepper. Cover, lower the heat, and simmer for 45 minutes; stir in chopped parsley and serve. Serves 6.

PEPPERS WITH CHICKEN ALLA PIEMONTESE

Peperoni con pollo alla Piemontese

1	4-pound stewing chicken, cut into pieces
4	ounces thinly sliced Italian prosciutto or bacon, diced
1	teaspoon rosemary leaves
6	tablespoons sweet butter or margarine, divided
3	bay leaves
1	cup homemade or canned chicken broth
1	cup dry white wine
6	large green or red peppers
3	tablespoons corn oil
5	anchovy fillets, finely chopped
2	cloves garlic, minced
4	tablespoons fresh lemon juice
½	teaspoon black pepper
	salt to taste

Wash chicken and pat dry with paper towels.

Sauté prosciutto with rosemary in 3 tablespoons of butter in a large skillet; add bay leaves. Add chicken and brown well on all sides; add broth and wine. Reduce heat; cover and simmer for 1 hour.

Meanwhile, cut peppers in half, lengthwise; remove seeds and pith and cut into 1-inch strips. Rinse and drain well.

Place peppers in another skillet with oil, anchovies, and garlic. Sauté over medium heat for 15 minutes, stirring occasionally.

Sprinkle chicken with pepper and lemon juice; taste for salt. Add cooked peppers; stir, cover, and simmer for 15 minutes. Serve hot. Serves 6 to 8.

SQUASH AND CHICKEN STEW

Pollo in umido con zucca

¼ cup flour
1 teaspoon salt
½ teaspoon white pepper
4 pounds broiler-fryer chicken, cut into serving pieces
4 tablespoons corn oil
2 medium onions, thinly sliced
1 clove garlic, minced
1 teaspoon crumbled dried marjoram
2 bay leaves
2 cups homemade or canned chicken broth
8 ounces fresh or canned plum tomatoes, chopped
½ cup dry white wine
3 pounds Butternut squash, pared, seeded, and cut into 1-inch cubes

Combine flour, salt, and pepper; dredge chicken pieces in flour mixture, and shake off any excess.

Heat oil in a large skillet; brown chicken pieces a few at a time; remove as they are ready and set aside. Add onion and garlic to oil remaining in skillet; cook over medium heat for 5 minutes. Add marjoram, bay leaves, broth, tomatoes, and wine to onion in skillet; stir and cook for 10 minutes. Return chicken to skillet; cover and cook over low heat for 30 minutes. Add squash; cover and cook for 15 minutes longer, or until chicken and squash are tender. Taste for additional salt and pepper and serve with cooked noodles. Serves 6 to 8.

FISH
Pesci

ARTICHOKES WITH FILLETS OF SOLE
Filetti di sogliola con carciofi

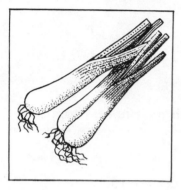

Serve with boiled or steamed rice and a tossed green salad.

10 ounces frozen or canned artichoke hearts, defrosted and well drained
 1 small onion, finely chopped
 6 sprigs fresh parsley, finely chopped
½ cup light cream, or
 1 cup low-fat yogurt plus 3 tablespoons nonfat dry skimmed milk powder
 4 tablespoons sweet butter or margarine
 2 tablespoons corn oil
1½ pounds fresh fillets of sole or any favorite fish fillets
¼ teaspoon salt
¼ teaspoon white pepper

Place artichoke hearts with the onion, parsley, and cream in the container of an electric blender or food processor. Cover and process for a few seconds, until sauce is smooth.

Pat fillets dry. Combine butter and oil in a large frying pan; sprinkle fillets with salt and pepper and place side by side in frying pan. Cook over medium heat for 2 minutes on each side. Pour sauce over fillets, lower the heat, and simmer for 5 minutes. Gently transfer fillets and sauce to a warm serving dish, and serve hot. Serves 6.

CAULIFLOWER WITH TUNA FISH
Cavolfiore con tonno al forno

Preheat oven to 400°F.

 1 cauliflower head, about 1½ pounds, or
20 ounces frozen cauliflower, defrosted, drained
 1 cup Béchamel sauce (see recipe, Chapter 5, Sauces)
½ cup wheat germ
14 ounces canned tuna fish, well drained

Remove and discard outer leaves and part of core from cauliflower. Steam in vegetable steamer over 1 inch salted water, covered, for 15 minutes. Drain well and transfer to a bake-and-serve dish.

Prepare Béchamel sauce.

Flake tuna fish and spread over cauliflower. Pour sauce over tuna and sprinkle with wheat germ. Bake for 10 minutes, or until lightly golden. Serve hot. Serves 6.

CODFISH WITH ONIONS
Merluzzo con cipolle

Delicious with hot polenta.

6 tablespoons corn oil
6 medium onions, thinly sliced
8 ounces canned plum tomatoes, with their juice, chopped
1 teaspoon salt
½ teaspoon black pepper
1 teaspoon dried marjoram
3 pounds fresh codfish, cut into serving pieces

Heat oil in a large saucepan; add onions; cook over low heat until onions are soft and golden. Add tomatoes, salt, pepper, and marjoram; stir and cook, uncovered, 15 minutes longer. Add fish; cover with sauce and onions. Cover saucepan and cook over low heat for 20 minutes. Taste for additional salt and pepper. Serves 6.

CUCUMBER SAUCE WITH TROUT
Salsa di cetrioli con trote

3 fresh crisp cucumbers
1 tablespoon minced onion
2 tablespoons chopped fresh chives
2 cups homemade mayonnaise (see recipe in Chapter 5, Sauces)
   salt
   pepper
6 trout, ½ pound each, poached and cooled

Peel cucumbers; remove seeds; slice very thin. Place in a strainer, sprinkle with ½ teaspoon salt, and set aside for 1 hour. Then rinse cucumbers well; place in a linen towel and squeeze out any liquid. Chop very fine.

In a small bowl combine chopped cucumbers, onion, chives, and mayonnaise; mix well. Taste for additional salt and pepper.

Arrange trout in a large serving platter; spoon cucumber sauce over to cover. Serve at room temperature. Serves 6.

FILLET OF SOLE WITH MUSHROOMS
Filetti di sogliola con funghi

A light and delicate way to serve fish.

Preheat oven to 400°F.
- 6 fillets of sole
- 5 tablespoons sweet butter or margarine
- 1 medium onion, thinly sliced
- 1 pound fresh firm mushrooms, sliced thin, or Shiitake mushrooms, sliced
- 1 cup dry white wine
- ½ teaspoon salt
- ¼ teaspoon white pepper
- 2 tablespoons chopped fresh parsley

Wash fillets and pat dry with paper towels. Melt 4 tablespoons butter in a skillet; add onion and sauté until soft. Add mushrooms and wine. Cook over medium heat until wine has evaporated; sprinkle with salt and pepper.

Arrange fillets on bottom of a well-buttered bake-and-serve dish. Pour mushrooms over fillets and sprinkle with parsley. Bake for 15 minutes. Serves 6.

FISH STEW WITH VEGETABLES

Zuppa di pesce con verdure

6 tablespoons olive oil
2 medium onions, finely chopped
2 cloves garlic, minced
2 large leeks, chopped
2 medium carrots, chopped
2 bay leaves, crumbled
4 sprigs fresh thyme, or
2 teaspoons dry thyme leaves
2 tablespoons chopped fresh parsley
¼ teaspoon saffron
1 teaspoon salt
1 teaspoon black pepper
1 cup dry white wine
6 ounces canned plum tomatoes, with their juice, chopped
1 pound fresh codfish
1 pound fresh haddock
1 pound fresh red snapper
3 dozen mussels, in shells, well scrubbed

Heat oil in a kettle; add onions, garlic, leeks, and carrots; cook, stirring occasionally, until onion is soft. Add bay leaves, thyme, parsley, saffron, salt, pepper, wine, and tomatoes. Bring to a boil; lower heat and cook uncovered for 10 minutes.

Cut fish into serving pieces; add to sauce and simmer for 5 minutes. Add mussels; continue cooking for 5 to 10 minutes, or until shells open. Taste for additional salt and pepper.

Transfer fish to individual warm serving soup bowls; pour some of the hot liquid over it and serve with some good crusty Italian bread. Serves 6.

7 Main Dishes
Cheese, Egg, Tarts, Molds *Piatti con*
Formaggi, uova, crostate, sformati

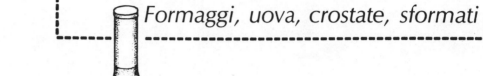

MILK

Butter

STUFFED VEGETABLES
Verdure ripiene

**ARTICHOKE-
FILLED CREPES**

Crespelle con carciofi

This recipe allows you to enjoy your guests. All elements can be prepared the day before, refrigerated, then baked.

Preheat oven to 400°F.

Crepes:
- 3 eggs
- 1 cup flour
- ½ teaspoon salt
- ¼ teaspoon white pepper
- 1 cup milk
- 3 tablespoons brandy
- 2 tablespoons oil

Béchamel sauce (see recipe in Chapter 5, Sauces)

Filling:
- 20 ounces frozen or canned artichoke hearts, defrosted and well drained, chopped
- ½ cup wheat germ
- 8 ounces fresh mushrooms, sliced thin
- ½ teaspoon thyme
- butter

To prepare crepes, beat eggs in a bowl until foamy, sift in flour mixed with salt and pepper and beat until smooth. Stir in milk, brandy, and oil.

Heat a 6-inch non-stick skillet, or a heavy crepe pan. Pour in one tablespoon of the batter and tilt the pan immediately so that the batter will cover the entire bottom of skillet. Cook crepes for 1 to 2 minutes on each side, until golden. Continue until all the batter is used. If crepes are made in advance, layer them with pieces of waxed paper in between and refrigerate. Makes about 20 crepes.

Prepare Béchamel sauce.

Filling: In a bowl combine chopped artichokes, wheat germ, mushrooms, thyme, and ½ cup Béchamel sauce; mix well. Taste for additional salt and pepper.

Spoon about 2 tablespoons filling into center of each crepe and roll up. Place each crepe seam side down in a buttered bake-and-serve dish. Pour remaining sauce over them, cover. Bake for 15 minutes. Serves 6 to 8.

BELGIAN ENDIVE WITH HAM
Indivia belga con prosciutto

An elegant luncheon dish.

Preheat broiler.

12	small heads Belgian endive
2	tablespoons sweet butter or margarine
1	lemon
¼	teaspoon salt
12	thin slices cooked ham
2	cups Béchamel sauce (see recipe in Chapter 5, Sauces)
½	cup grated Parmesan or Asiago cheese
	oil

Remove and discard any discolored outer leaves from endives; place remaining leaves in a single layer in a large skillet. Add enough water to cover bottom of pan. Add 2 tablespoons butter and the juice of 1 lemon; sprinkle with the salt. Cover and cook over medium heat for 20 minutes. Drain well.

Spread each slice of ham with some of the Béchamel sauce; wrap one slice of ham around each endive. Arrange endive rolls side by side in a well-oiled bake-and-serve dish. Cover with remaining sauce; sprinkle with the grated cheese. Broil until lightly browned. Serves 6.

STUFFED EGGPLANT ROLLS
Involtini di melanzane

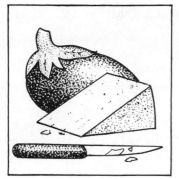

Preheat oven to 375°F.

2 eggplants, about 2 pounds
1½ cups ground or chopped ham
1 cup grated Gruyère or Swiss cheese
2 tablespoons chopped fresh parsley
2 cups Béchamel sauce (see recipe in Chapter 5, Sauces)
2 eggs, lightly beaten

Peel eggplant and cut across into ¼-inch round slices. Place on a greased baking sheet and broil under preheated broiler for 3 minutes on each side. Set aside.

In a bowl, combine chopped ham, grated cheese, parsley, and 4 tablespoons Béchamel sauce. Mix well with a wooden spoon. Spoon some of the ham mixture onto each slice of eggplant and roll up.

Arrange eggplant rolls in a bake-and-serve dish, side by side, with seam side down. Spread Béchamel sauce over rolls. Bake for 10 to 15 minutes. Serve hot. Serves 6.

JERUSALEM ARTICHOKE CROQUETTES
Polpettine di topinambur

2 pounds fresh and firm Jerusalem artichokes
1 large potato, peeled, diced
3 tablespoons chopped fresh parsley or chives
3 eggs
1 cup wheat germ
1 teaspoon salt
¼ teaspoon white pepper
1 cup unflavored bread crumbs
oil for deep drying

Scrub artichokes and potato with a vegetable brush; rinse well. Place artichokes and peeled, diced potato in a vegetable steamer with 1 inch salted water; cover and steam for 10 minutes, or until fork tender. Cool long enough to handle, then peel artichokes. Place artichokes and potatoes in container of electric blender or food processor and puree. Transfer to a mixing bowl. Add chopped parsley, wheat germ, 2 beaten eggs, salt, and pepper; mix well.

Beat remaining egg. Shape a tablespoon of puree mixture into an egg-shaped croquette and dip into egg, then into bread crumbs. Repeat process until batter is used. Shake off excess and refrigerate for 1 hour.

Heat oil in deep fryer or heavy skillet. Sauté croquettes over medium-high heat until golden on all sides; drain on paper towels and serve hot. Serves 6.

JERUSALEM ARTICHOKES ALLA TORINESE
Topinambur alla Torinese

3 pounds fresh and firm Jerusalem artichokes
4 tablespoons sweet butter or margarine
6 eggs
2 tablespoons chopped fresh parsley
1 clove garlic, minced
½ teaspoon salt
6 thin slices Fontina or Fontinella cheese

Scrape artichokes with a vegetable brush, rinse well. Place in vegetable steamer over 1 inch simmering salted water. Cover and steam for 6 minutes. Cool long enough to handle, then peel. Cut into 1-inch cubes.

Melt butter in skillet, and, over low heat, cook artichokes until lightly golden, stirring occasionally.

In the meantime soft-cook eggs. Bring water to a boil; place egg on a spoon and lower into boiling water; cook for about 3 to 5 minutes. Remove immediately from hot water, and plunge into cold water. Peel, and very gently cut each egg in half. The yolks will be soft, so be careful.

Transfer artichokes to a warm serving dish; sprinkle with chopped parsley combined with garlic and pepper. Arrange sliced cheese over artichokes and place egg halves on top. Serve immediately. Serves 6.

STUFFED CABBAGE ROLLS
Indoltini di cavolo

Preheat oven to 350°F.
1   medium Savoy cabbage
1   pound sweet Italian sausage, skinned and crumbled
½   cup uncooked rice
3   tablespoons chopped fresh parsley
4   sage leaves, crumbled
½   teaspoon dried marjoram
½   cup wheat germ or unflavored bread crumbs
2   eggs, lightly beaten
4   tablespoons grated Parmesan or Asiago cheese
2   teaspoons salt
½   teaspoon black pepper
3   tablespoons corn oil
1   cup tomato sauce
2   cups homemade or canned beef broth
½   cup dry white wine
2   bay leaves

Place washed cabbage in large saucepan. Cover with boiling water; add 1 teaspoon salt; bring to a boil and cook for 5 minutes. Cool in water. Drain and carefully remove 12 outer leaves. Set flat on cutting board; remove hard stems and set aside. In a bowl combine sausage meat, uncooked rice, parsley, sage, marjoram, wheat germ, eggs, cheese, remaining teaspoon salt, and pepper. Work mixture with hands until well blended. Place some stuffing on prepared leaves. Form rolls by folding side of leaf over stuffing and rolling. Set aside. (If stuffing is left over use more leaves.) Slice remaining cabbage. Heat oil in Dutch oven; add sliced cabbage, tomato sauce, broth, wine, bay leaves. Bring to a boil and cook uncovered for 5 minutes. Arrange cabbage rolls side by side on top of cabbage in Dutch oven. Cover; bake for one hour. Remove cover and bake 10 minutes longer. Serves 6.

STUFFED PEPPER ALLA PIEMONTESE
Peperoni ripieni alla Piemontese

Preheat oven to 375°F.

- 3 large green or red peppers
- 4 medium zucchini
- 3 tablespoons corn oil
- 4 tablespoons sweet butter or margarine
- ½ teaspoon salt
- ½ teaspoon white pepper
- 6 eggs
- 8 ounces Fontina or Fontinella cheese, diced
- ½ cup water

Rinse peppers and zucchini. Cut peppers in half, lengthwise; remove seeds and pith. Remove ends from zucchini and cut in half, lengthwise. Place peppers and zucchini in vegetable steamer over simmering salted water. Cover and steam for 8 minutes. Drain; set aside.

Dice zucchini and place in a frying pan with the oil and 2 tablespoons butter; sprinkle with salt and pepper. Beat eggs, pour over zucchini, and cook over medium heat for 3 minutes, stirring constantly. Remove from heat and stir in diced cheese. Spoon mixture into pepper halves.

Arrange peppers in a shallow baking dish; dot with remaining butter. Add ½ cup water to baking dish. Bake for 15 minutes. Serve hot. Serves 6.

MEAT AND MUSHROOM STUFFED POTATOES
Patate ripiene

Preheat oven to 400°F.

- 6 large baking potatoes
- 3 tablespoons sweet butter or margarine
- 3 tablespoons corn oil
- 1 clove garlic, mashed
- 8 ounces sausage meat, crumbled
- 1 egg, beaten
- 4 tablespoons chopped fresh parsley
- 8 ounces fresh mushrooms, thinly sliced
- 1 teaspoon marjoram
- 1 teaspoon salt
- ½ teaspoon black pepper

Bake potatoes with their skins for 45 minutes, or until fork tender. Remove from oven, cut in half lengthwise; scoop out potato, being careful not to break the skin. Mash the potato and set aside.

Melt butter in a skillet; add oil and garlic and sauté until garlic is golden, then remove and discard. In the remaining fat in skillet add crumbled sausage; cook and stir until nicely browned. Remove sausage with slotted spoon onto paper towel to drain. Add sausage to mashed potatoes. Add beaten egg and parsley to sausage and potato mixture. Reserve fat.

Sauté mushrooms in fat in skillet for 5 minutes with marjoram, salt, and pepper. Drain; add to mashed potatoes and mix well. Return mixture to potato skins in a baking pan. Bake potatoes for 15 minutes. Gently transfer to a warm serving dish and serve. Serves 6.

STUFFED ZUCCHINI ALLA PIEMONTESE

Zucchine ripiene alla Piemontese

Preheat oven to 375°F.

6 medium size zucchini, about 7 to 8 inches long
1 pound chicken breast or thigh, skinned, boned, and chopped
3 shallots, chopped
½ clove garlic, minced
1 tablespoon chopped fresh basil
2 anchovy fillets, chopped
2 eggs, slightly beaten
3 tablespoons melted butter or margarine
3 tablespoons unflavored bread crumbs

Remove ends from zucchini and steam for 10 minutes. Set aside to cool.

In a bowl combine chicken, shallots, garlic, basil, anchovies, and eggs; mix well. Taste for salt.

Cut zucchini lengthwise through the center and carefully scoop out seeds and some of the pulp to make a boatlike form. Save pulp for a soup. Fill each boat with some of the chicken mixture; dribble melted butter over it and sprinkle with bread crumbs. Bake for 25 minutes. Serve hot or at room temperature. Serves 6.

CHEESE DISHES
Piatti con formaggi

**ARTICHOKES
WITH TWO
CHEESES**

*Carciofi ai due
formaggi*

Serve as you would a soufflé.

Preheat oven to 350°F.

6 medium artichokes
1 lemon, sliced
6 ounces Fontina cheese, diced
4 tablespoons grated Parmesan or Asiago cheese
6 tablespoons wheat germ
2 tablespoons chopped fresh basil, or
2 teaspoons dried basil
2 eggs, slightly beaten
½ teaspoon white pepper
   salt to taste
6 anchovy fillets, cut in half lengthwise
1 cup warm water

To prepare artichokes, see recipe for Marinated Artichoke Hearts, Chapter 2.

Rub the cut part of artichokes with a lemon slice. Place in steam basket and steam over 1 inch of salted water for 18 to 20 minutes. Drain and set aside.

In a bowl, combine Fontina and Parmesan cheese, wheat germ, basil, eggs, and pepper; mix well and taste for salt. Fill artichokes with mixture, rounding up filling to a dome-shaped top. Garnish each with two pieces of anchovy fillets, placing them in the shape of a cross.

Arrange artichokes in a single layer in well-oiled shallow baking pan. Pour 1 cup warm water in pan. Bake for 1 hour. Transfer very gently to a warm serving dish and serve hot. Serves 6.

ASPARAGUS OPEN-FACED SANDWICH
Crostoni di asparagi

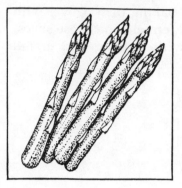

An excellent luncheon dish if accompanied by a tomato salad.

36 fresh asparagus, or
36 frozen or canned asparagus spears, defrosted and well drained
12 slices thick bread of your choice
 6 tablespoons sweet butter or margarine
12 thin slices of Fontina or American cheese
 1 teaspoon caraway seed
12 eggs, fried
 4 tablespoons grated Parmesan or Asiago cheese
    pepper to taste

To prepare fresh asparagus, see recipe for Asparagus and Prosciutto Rolls, Chapter 2.

Remove crust from bread, toast, and spread with the butter.

Drain asparagus well. Place 3 asparagus spears on each slice of toast; top with a slice of cheese and sprinkle with caraway seed. Place under the broiler until cheese is soft but not melted. Place a fried egg over each slice, sprinkle with Parmesan cheese, and pepper. Serve hot. Serves 6.

FENNELS WITH CHEESE
Finocchi al formaggio

A light luncheon dish.

Preheat oven to 350°F.
 6 medium fennels
12 slices Fontina or Fontinella cheese
 4 tablespoons sweet butter or margarine
⅛ teaspoon nutmeg
½ cup grated Parmesan or Asiago cheese

Remove and discard tops and tough outer leaves of fennels. Cut in half and then cut each half into ¼-inch-thick slices. Rinse well.

Place in vegetable steamer over 1 inch simmering salted water. Cover and steam for 15 minutes. Drain. Arrange one layer of sliced fennel in a well-buttered shallow baking dish. Cover with sliced Fontina cheese; repeat with sliced fennel and cheese slices. Dot final layer with butter, sprinkle with nutmeg and grated cheese. Bake for 15 minutes. Serve hot. Serves 6.

BAKED MUSHROOM WITH CHEESE TORINESE-STYLE
Funghi al forno con Fontina alla Torinese

The original recipe would use *porcini* (wild mushrooms from the woods), but it is also good with the cultivated kind. Shiitake mushrooms are closer in flavor to the wild variety.

Preheat oven to 375°F.
2 pounds fresh firm mushrooms
6 tablespoons sweet butter or margarine
1 teaspoon salt
½ teaspoon white pepper
8 ounces Fontina or Fontinella cheese, shredded

Wash mushrooms and pat dry with paper towels. Cut in slices about ¼ inch thick, lengthwise, from cap to stem.

Melt butter in a skillet; add mushrooms a few at a time and sauté for 5 minutes. Sprinkle with salt and pepper. Arrange sautéed mushrooms in layers, in a bake-and-serve dish, alternating with shredded cheese. Continue until all the mushrooms and cheese have been used. Finish with a layer of cheese.

Cover and bake for 15 minutes. Serve hot. Serves 6.

SQUASH AND CHEESE CASSEROLE

Zucca al forno con formaggio

Can be served with roast turkey or ham.

Preheat broiler.

- 3 pounds Butternut squash or pumpkin
- 3 cups milk
- 2 beef bouillon cubes, crumbled
- 4 tablespoons water
- 4 tablespoons sweet butter or margarine
- 4 eggs, separated
- 1/2 cup grated Parmesan or Asiago cheese
- 1/2 teaspoon salt
- 1/2 teaspoon white pepper
- 1/4 teaspoon nutmeg
- 1/2 cup seedless raisins, soaked and drained
- 8 ounces sliced Fontina or Fontinella cheese, cut into strips
  oil

To prepare squash, rinse, peel, seed, and cut into cubes.

Place cubes in a large saucepan; add milk, crumbled bouillon cubes, and 4 tablespoons water. Bring to a boil; reduce heat, and cook until squash is soft. Transfer squash with a slotted spoon to a blender or food processor and puree.

Return squash to saucepan and cook until all the milk has been absorbed. Stir from time to time to avoid squash sticking to bottom of saucepan. Remove from heat; cool to lukewarm. Add slightly beaten egg yolks, grated cheese, salt, pepper, nutmeg, and raisins; stir well to mix.

Beat egg whites until stiff; gently fold into squash mixture. Spoon mixture into a well-oiled baking dish; arrange sliced cheese on top of squash; dot with butter. Broil until cheese has melted. Serves 6.

EGG DISHES
Piatti con uova

NOTE: If you use a non-stick 10-inch frying pan you will have no problem turning the frittata.

FRITTATA WITH ARTICHOKES

Frittata con carciofi

Quick to prepare.

4	medium artichokes
1	lemon
4	tablespoons corn oil
1	large onion, thinly sliced
½	cup dry white wine
6	eggs
1	teaspoon salt
¼	teaspoon white pepper
¼	teaspoon dry marjoram

To prepare artichokes, see recipe for Marinated Artichoke Hearts, Chapter 2. Before placing in bowl with lemon juice, cut each artichoke into 4 wedges, then cut each wedge into ⅛-inch-thick slices, lengthwise.

Heat oil in frying pan; add onion and well-drained artichokes; sprinkle with the wine, cover, and simmer for 15 minutes. Do not let dry; if necessary add a few tablespoons of water. Beat eggs with salt, pepper, and marjoram, pour over artichokes; stir and cook over low heat until mixture begins to set.

Remove pan from heat, place a plate upside down over *frittata*, and holding plate and pan closely together, turn pan quickly upside down over the plate. Slip the frittata, cooked side up, from plate into frying pan; and do not stir this time, but cook for 3 to 4 minutes. Slide it back on plate and serve. Good hot or cold. Serves 4 to 6.

FRITTATA WITH ASPARAGUS
Frittata di asparagi

Good hot or cold.

 1 pound fresh asparagus, or
10 ounces frozen or canned asparagus spears, defrosted and well drained, cut into 2-inch pieces
 3 tablespoons sweet butter or margarine
 6 eggs
 1 teaspoon salt
 ¼ teaspoon white pepper
 ¼ teaspoon nutmeg
 4 tablespoons Parmesan or Asiago cheese

To prepare fresh asparagus, see recipe for Asparagus and Prosciutto Rolls, Chapter 2.

Over medium heat, melt butter in frying pan, cook cut asparagus spears for 5 minutes. Beat eggs with salt, pepper, nutmeg, and cheese; pour over asparagus; stir and cook over low heat until mixture begins to set.

Remove from heat, and follow procedure for turning and serving *frittate* in recipe for Frittata with Artichokes. Serves 4 to 6.

CARROT AND CHEESE FRITTATA
Frittata di carote e formaggio

With just a nice salad added, you have a very satisfactory summer meal.

 1 pound fresh carrots, or
10 ounces frozen cut carrots, defrosted, drained
 3 tablespoons corn oil
 ½ teaspoon crumbled rosemary leaves
 6 eggs
 ¼ teaspoon white pepper
 ½ teaspoon salt
 6 ounces Fontina or Fontinella cheese, diced

Scrape fresh carrots and cut into ¼-inch-thick slices; rinse and drain well. Place in a vegetable steamer over 1 inch salted water, cover and steam for 6 minutes. Drain well.

Heat oil in frying pan, add crumbled rosemary leaves and carrots; cook over medium heat for 6 to 8 minutes, or until carrots are fork tender. The time depends on the size of the carrots.

Beat eggs with salt and pepper; add diced cheese and pour over carrots. Stir and cook over low heat until mixture begins to set.

Remove pan from heat, and follow procedure for turning and serving *frittata* in recipe for Frittata with Artichokes earlier in this chapter. Serves 6.

EGGPLANT FRITTATA
Frittata di melanzane

Preheat broiler.

1	medium eggplant, about 1 pound
6	eggs
1	teaspoon salt
½	teaspoon pepper
4	tablespoons grated Parmesan or Asiago cheese
3	tablespoons corn oil
3	tablespoons sweet butter or margarine
1	clove garlic, mashed

Peel eggplant, cut into ¼-inch-thick round slices. Place on a greased baking sheet and broil, about 5 inches from heat, for 5 minutes; turn over eggplant slices and broil 2 minutes longer. (You may do this early in the day, and have the eggplants ready to use for dinnertime).

Beat eggs with salt, pepper, and grated cheese. Heat oil in frying pan; add butter and garlic; fry garlic until it turns golden, then discard it. Place half of eggplant slices in frying pan, pour beaten eggs over, then arrange remaining eggplant slices on top. Cook over low heat until mixture begins to set.

Remove from heat, and follow procedure for turning and serving *frittate* in recipe for Frittata with Artichokes earlier in this chapter. Serves 6.

ENDIVE FRITTATA
Frittata di indivia

1 medium head endive lettuce, about 1½ pounds
3 tablespoons oil
6 eggs
1 teaspoon salt
¼ teaspoon white pepper
2 tablespoons chopped fresh or frozen and defrosted chives

Wash endive; remove and discard the hard ribs from leaves. Shred remaining endive and place in vegetable steamer with 1 inch salted water. Cover and steam for 6 minutes. Drain and squeeze out any excess water.

Heat oil in frying pan; add chopped endive and cook over medium heat for 5 minutes.

Beat eggs with salt, pepper, and chives. Pour over endive and stir and cook over low heat until mixture begins to set. Remove from heat, and follow procedure for turning and serving *frittate* in recipe for Frittata with Artichokes earlier in this chapter. Serves 6.

FENNEL FRITTATA
Frittata di finocchi

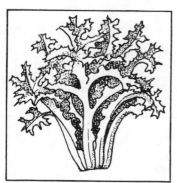

2 small fennels
4 tablespoons sweet butter or margarine
6 eggs
½ teaspoon salt
¼ teaspoon white pepper
½ cup grated Parmesan or Asiago cheese

To prepare fennels, remove tops and tough outer leaves and discard; cut each fennel in half, then cut into ¼-inch-thick slices. Rinse well. Place in vegetable steamer with 1 inch salted water. Cover and steam for 15 minutes. Drain well.

Melt butter in frying pan; add fennels and cook over medium heat for 6 to 8 minutes. Beat eggs with salt, pepper, and grated cheese; pour mixture over fennels; stir and cook over low heat until mixture begins to set.

Remove pan from heat, and follow procedure for turning and serving *frittate* in recipe for Frittata with Artichokes earlier in this chapter. Serves 6.

MUSHROOM FRITTATA
Frittata di funghi

Delightful dish for brunch or luncheon.

3 tablespoons corn oil
1 small onion, thinly sliced
8 ounces fresh firm mushrooms, cleaned, thinly sliced
6 eggs
2 tablespoons chopped fresh basil or parsley
½ cup grated Swiss cheese
½ teaspoon salt
¼ teaspoon white pepper

Heat oil in frying pan; add onion and sauté until onion is soft. Add sliced mushrooms and sauté for 4 minutes. Beat eggs with basil or parsley, grated cheese, salt, and pepper; pour over mushrooms; stir and cook over low heat until mixture begins to set.

Remove from heat, and follow procedure for turning and serving *frittate* in recipe for Frittata with Artichokes earlier in this chapter. Serves 6.

ONION FRITTATA
Frittata di cipolle

Very good cold, with a sprinkle of wine vinegar.

4 tablespoons olive oil
4 large onions, thinly sliced
6 eggs
½ cup grated Parmesan or Asiago cheese
½ teaspoon salt
½ teaspoon white pepper

Heat oil in frying pan; add onions and sauté over medium heat until golden and soft. Beat eggs with cheese, salt, and pepper; pour over onions; stir and cook over low heat until mixture begins to set.

Remove pan from heat, and follow procedure for turning and serving *frittata* in recipe for Frittata with Artichokes earlier in this chapter. Serves 6.

MINTED PEA FRITTATA
Frittata di piselli con menta

For this you may use frozen peas, with good results.

4 tablespoons corn oil
10 ounces frozen peas, defrosted, drained
6 eggs
4 ounces shredded Fontina or Fontinella cheese
4 tablespoons grated Parmesan or Asiago cheese
1 tablespoon chopped fresh mint, or
1 teaspoon dried mint
½ teaspoon salt
¼ teaspoon white pepper

Heat oil in frying pan; add defrosted and well-drained peas, and cook over medium heat for 5 minutes. Beat eggs with Fontina and Parmesan cheese; add mint, salt, and pepper. Pour over peas; stir and cook over low heat until mixture begins to set.

Remove pan from heat, and follow procedure for turning and serving *frittate* in recipe for Frittata with Artichokes earlier in this chapter. Serves 6.

PEPPER FRITTATA
Frittata di peperoni

3 to 5 tablespoons corn oil
3 tablespoons sweet butter or margarine
1 large clove garlic, sliced
2 medium green peppers
2 medium red peppers (if you cannot find red peppers, use 4 green peppers)
6 eggs
½ teaspoon salt
½ teaspoon white pepper
4 tablespoons grated Swiss cheese
1 teaspoon anchovy paste
3 slices white bread, crust removed, cubed

Heat 3 tablespoons oil and 3 tablespoons butter in frying pan; add garlic and sauté for 5 minutes, or until golden; remove garlic and discard.

Cut peppers in half lengthwise; remove seeds and pith; cut into 1-inch strips; rinse and drain well.

Add peppers to fat in frying pan and, over medium heat, cook uncovered for 25 minutes; stir occasionally.

Meanwhile, combine eggs with salt, pepper, and grated cheese; beat well and set aside.

When peppers are cooked, remove from pan and set aside.

Add anchovy paste to fat remaining in pan; add bread cubes and stir over high heat for 2 minutes. If necessary, add 1 or 2 tablespoons of corn oil to pan. Return peppers to pan; stir; add beaten egg mixture; stir and cook over low heat until mixture begins to set.

Remove from heat, and follow procedure for turning and serving *frittate* in recipe for Frittata with Artichokes earlier in this chapter. Serves 6.

POTATO FRITTATA
Frittata di patate

3	medium potatoes, about 1 pound, peeled, diced
3	tablespoons corn oil
3	tablespoons sweet butter or margarine
½	teaspoon crumbled dried rosemary leaves
1	clove garlic, minced
6	eggs
1	teaspoon salt
¼	teaspoon white pepper
4	tablespoons grated Parmesan or Asiago cheese

Bring a saucepan of salted water to a boil; drop diced potatoes in and boil for 4 minutes. Drain immediately.

Heat oil and butter and add rosemary and garlic; sauté for 4 minutes. Add drained potatoes; stir and cook for 5 minutes.

Beat eggs with salt, pepper, and grated cheese; pour over potatoes; stir and cook over low heat until mixture begins to set. Remove pan from heat, and follow procedure for turning and serving *frittate* in recipe for Frittata with Artichokes earlier in this chapter. Serves 6.

SOYBEAN SPROUT FRITTATA

Frittata di germogli di soia

3 tablespoons corn oil
1 pound soybean sprouts
1 clove garlic, minced
6 eggs
4 tablespoons grated Parmesan or Asiago cheese
½ teaspoon salt
½ teaspoon white pepper

Heat oil in frying pan; add sprouts and garlic, and cook over medium heat for 6 to 8 minutes, until sprouts are soft. Beat eggs with grated cheese, salt, and pepper; pour over sprouts; stir and cook over low heat until mixture begins to set.

Remove pan from heat, and follow procedure for turning and serving *frittate* in recipe for Frittata with Artichokes earlier in this chapter. Serves 4 to 6.

SPINACH AND BACON FRITTATA

Frittata di spinaci con pancetta

3 pounds fresh spinach, or
30 ounces frozen chopped spinach, thawed and drained
4 tablespoons corn oil
6 slices bacon, diced
1 small onion, chopped
1 clove garlic, minced
6 eggs
1 teaspoon salt
¼ teaspoon black pepper
½ cup grated Parmesan or Asiago cheese

To prepare fresh spinach remove roots and hard stems. Place spinach in vegetable steamer with 1 inch salted water. Cover and steam for 5 minutes. Drain and squeeze out any excess water. Chop.

Heat oil in frying pan; add bacon and cook until crisp; stir in onions and garlic and cook for 5 minutes. Stir in drained spinach, and cook for 5 minutes longer.

Beat eggs with salt, pepper, and grated cheese; pour over spinach; stir and cook over low heat until mixture begins to set. Remove pan from heat, and follow procedure for turning and serving *frittate* in recipe for Frittata with Artichokes earlier in this chapter. Serves 6.

SPINACH FRITTATA WITH ONIONS

Frittata di spinaci con cipolla

This recipe came to me by accident. I wanted to make a spinach *frittata*, but did not have enough spinach, so I added onions, and created a delightful surprise.

2 pounds fresh spinach, or
20 ounces frozen chopped spinach, thawed and well drained
4 tablespoons corn oil
4 medium onions, thinly sliced
6 eggs
1 teaspoon salt
½ teaspoon black pepper
¼ teaspoon nutmeg

To prepare fresh spinach see preceding recipe for Spinach and Bacon Frittata.

Heat oil in frying pan and add onions; cook until soft. Stir in spinach and cook over low heat for 5 minutes. Beat eggs with salt, pepper, and nutmeg; pour over spinach; stir and cook over low heat until mixture begins to set.

Remove pan from heat, and follow procedure for turning and serving *frittate* in recipe for Frittata with Artichokes earlier in this chapter. Serves 6.

TOMATO-ANCHOVY FRITTATA

Frittata di pomodori e acciughe

16 ounces canned plum tomatoes, well drained
4 tablespoons corn oil
6 anchovy fillets, chopped
6 fresh basil leaves, or
2 tablespoons chopped fresh parsley
6 eggs
¼ teaspoon white pepper
  salt

Cut drained tomatoes in slices.

Heat oil in frying pan and stir in anchovies and basil; cook over low heat for 3 minutes. Add tomatoes, stir and cook for 5 minutes.

Beat eggs with pepper, and if you desire, a little salt; pour over tomatoes; stir and cook over low heat until mixture begins to set. Remove from heat, and follow procedure for turning and serving *frittate* in recipe for Frittata with Artichokes earlier in this chapter. Serves 6.

ZUCCHINI FRITTATA

Frittata di zucchine

Good hot, or cold with a sprinkle of wine vinegar.

4 fresh zucchini, about 8 inches long
4 tablespoons corn oil
1 teaspoon salt
½ teaspoon white pepper
6 eggs
½ cup grated Parmesan or Asiago cheese

Wash zucchini; remove both ends and discard. Cut into very thin slices.

Heat oil in frying pan; add zucchini and cook over medium heat for 5 minutes; zucchini should not be mushy. Sprinkle with salt and pepper.

Beat eggs with grated cheese; pour over zucchini; stir and cook over low heat until mixture begins to set. Remove pan from heat, and follow procedure for turning and serving *frittate* in recipe for Frittata with Artichokes earlier in this chapter. Serves 6.

TARTS
Crostate

ARTICHOKE TART
Crostata di carciofi

Can be prepared ahead of time and baked at the last minute. May be used as an appetizer, also, in which case it could serve up to 12 people.

Preheat oven to 400°F.

Pastry:
- 2 cups flour
- ¾ cup butter or margarine, at room temperature
- ½ teaspoon salt
- 2 whole eggs
- ¼ teaspoon white pepper
- ⅛ teaspoon nutmeg
  butter and flour for baking pan
- 1 egg yolk
- 2 tablespoons cold water

Filling:
- 3 tablespoons butter
- 30 ounces frozen or canned artichoke hearts, defrosted and well drained
- 1 small onion, grated
- 2 tablespoons chopped fresh parsley
- ½ teaspoon dried marjoram
- 4 ounces Fontina cheese, diced
- 4 ounces Mozzarella cheese, diced
- 4 ounces grated Parmesan or Asiago cheese
- 4 eggs, slightly beaten
- 1 cup light cream, or
- 1 cup low-fat yogurt plus 2 tablespoons nonfat dry milk powder

To prepare pastry, in a bowl combine flour, butter, salt, eggs, pepper, and nutmeg. Work mixture with your hands until mixed well; shape into a smooth ball; cover and refrigerate for at least 30 minutes. You may use a food processor and process until mixture forms a ball.

Divide dough in two. Roll one half on a lightly floured surface into a 12-inch circle, ⅛ inch thick; gently transfer to a buttered and floured 10-inch fluted pie pan. Prick bottom of dough with fork. Bake for 10 minutes. Remove from oven and set aside.

To prepare filling, heat butter in skillet, add artichokes and onion; sauté for 5 minutes. Stir in parsley and marjoram and remove from heat. Add Fontina, Mozzarella, and grated Parmesan cheese, stir in eggs and cream, fold gently to mix.

Pour filling into baked shell. Roll out second half of pastry. Cut into narrow strips; weave in lattice fashion over filling. Trim ends. Moisten edge of bottom crust. With fingers, press down strips at edge. Beat egg yolk with cold water and gently brush over strips. Bake for 20 minutes. Serve hot. Serves 6 to 8.

ASPARAGUS TART
Crostata di asparagi

Very good as a main dish for a light meal.

Preheat oven to 400°F.
Pastry:
1   cup flour
4   tablespoons sweet butter or margarine, at room temperature
¼   teaspoon salt
1   whole egg
⅛   teaspoon white pepper
⅛   teaspoon nutmeg
     butter and flour for baking pan

Filling:
60   fresh asparagus, or
60   frozen or canned asparagus spears, defrosted, and well drained
1   tablespoon butter or margarine
1   tablespoon flour
1   cup light cream, or
1   cup low-fat yogurt plus 2 tablespoons nonfat dry milk powder
⅛   teaspoon nutmeg
4   tablespoons grated Parmesan or Asiago cheese
4   tablespoons grated Gruyère or Swiss cheese

To prepare fresh asparagus, see recipe for Asparagus and Pros-ciutto Rolls, Chapter 2. Drain well and keep warm.

To prepare pastry, in a bowl combine flour, butter, salt, pepper, and nutmeg. Work mixture with your hands until mixed. Shape into a smooth ball; cover and refrigerate for at least 30 minutes. You may use a food processor and process until mixture forms a ball.

Remove dough from refrigerator; roll on a lightly floured surface into a 12-inch circle, ⅛ inch thick; gently transfer to a buttered and floured 10-inch fluted pie pan. Prick the bottom of dough with fork. Bake for 20 minutes, or until lightly golden. Remove from oven and set aside.

To prepare filling, melt butter over low heat in a small saucepan; stir in flour and cream and continue stirring; bring to a boil and remove immediately from heat; stir in nutmeg and cheese until melted.

Pour cheese sauce into prepared shell; arrange well-drained asparagus on top and warm in a 400°F oven for 5 minutes. Serves 6 to 8.

BROCCOLI TART
Crostata di broccoli

Preheat oven to 400°F.

1 recipe for pastry (see Artichoke Tart recipe earlier in this chapter)
1 bunch fresh broccoli, about 1½ pounds, or
20 ounces frozen chopped broccoli, defrosted and drained
1 cup minced onions
4 ounces fresh mushrooms, sliced
1 teaspoon salt
¼ teaspoon black pepper
⅛ teaspoon nutmeg
1 cup light cream, or
1 cup low-fat yogurt plus 2 tablespoons nonfat dry milk powder
3 eggs, slightly beaten

Prepare pastry.

To prepare filling, discard outer leaves of broccoli; cut off the lower part of stalks. Place in a vegetable steamer with 1 inch of salted water and steam for 6 minutes. Drain and chop coarsely. Transfer to a mixing bowl; add chopped onions, mushrooms, salt, pepper, nutmeg, cream, and beaten eggs; fold gently to mix.

Proceed as in Artichoke Tart recipe. Serves 6 to 8.

LEEK TART
Crostata di porri

Preheat oven to 400°F.

1   recipe for pastry (see Asparagus Tart recipe earlier in this chapter) plus 2 tablespoons sweet butter
6   large leeks
4   eggs
1   cup light cream, or
1   cup low-fat yogurt plus 2 tablespoons non-fat dry milk powder
6   ounces Fontina or Fontinella cheese, shredded
6   ounces baked ham, diced
½   teaspoon white pepper
    salt to taste

Prepare pastry.

To prepare leeks, see recipe for Leeks with Caper Sauce, Chapter 2. Place in a vegetable steamer with 1 inch salted water. Cover and steam for 15 minutes. Drain.

Beat eggs with cream; add shredded cheese, diced ham, pepper, and taste for salt. Spread drained leeks in bottom of crust; pour egg mixture over leeks. Bake for 25 to 30 minutes, or until firm. Serve hot or cold. Serves 6.

MUSHROOM TART

Crostata di funghi

Very good as a luncheon dish or as an appetizer.

Preheat oven to 400°F.

 1 recipe for pastry (see Artichoke Tart recipe in this chapter) minus 1 tablespoon water
 4 tablespoons sweet butter or margarine
 2 pounds fresh mushrooms, washed and sliced
 1 tablespoon flour
 ½ cup dry white wine
 1 teaspoon salt
 ½ teaspoon white pepper
 ½ cup homemade or canned beef broth
 2 egg yolks

Prepare pastry.

In a skillet, over medium heat, melt butter; sauté mushrooms for 5 minutes; stir in flour; add wine, salt, pepper, broth, and egg yolks. Stir well, return to low heat and cook, stirring, for 10 minutes. Pour mushrooms into baked shell.

Proceed as in recipe for Artichoke Tart. Bake for 10 minutes, or until golden. Serves 6.

ONION TART

Crostata di cipolle

Preheat oven to 400°F.

 1 recipe for pastry (see Asparagus Tart recipe earlier in this chapter), without butter
 4 tablespoons corn oil
 6 medium onions, peeled and thinly sliced
 1 cup homemade or canned beef broth
 2 cups Béchamel sauce (see recipe in Chapter 5, Sauces)
 8 slices lean bacon
 2 eggs, beaten

Prepare pastry.

To prepare filling, heat oil in a skillet, add onions and sauté until golden and soft; add broth, cover and cook over low heat for 15 minutes.

In the meantime cook bacon until nicely crisp; drain on paper towels and arrange side by side in bottom of prepared crust.

Drain onions if necessary; add to Béchamel sauce; stir in beaten eggs, then pour mixture over bacon in crust. Bake in 350°F oven for 35 minutes. Serve hot. Serves 6.

PEAS AND CARROTS TART

Crostata di piselli e carote

Preheat oven to 400°F.
Pastry:
2   cups flour
¾   cup butter, at room temperature
½   teaspoon salt
2   whole eggs
     butter and flour for baking pan
     dried beans

Filling:
2   cups Béchamel sauce (see recipe in Chapter 5, Sauces)
¼   cup grated Gruyère or Swiss cheese
4   tablespoons butter or margarine
1   teaspoon rosemary leaves
1   clove garlic, sliced
½   teaspoon salt
4   green celery ribs, parboiled for 5 minutes
1   pound fresh carrots, peeled and diced
1   pound fresh peas, or
1   10-ounce package frozen peas, thawed

To prepare pastry crust, see recipe for Asparagus Tart earlier in this chapter, using above ingredients. (Before baking crust, cover the bottom of pie crust with aluminum foil and cover that with dried beans, to prevent crust from puffing up.)

Make Béchamel sauce. Remove from heat, stir in grated cheese and set aside.

In a small saucepan, melt 4 tablespoons butter; add rosemary leaves, garlic, and salt; sauté at medium heat for 5 minutes. Spoon Béchamel sauce into baked crust; arrange celery ribs across top to form eight wedges. Fill four with carrots and four with peas. Strain the melted butter over peas and carrots, discarding rosemary and garlic.

Bake for 10 minutes. Serve hot. Serves 6 to 8.

POTATO TART
Crostata di patate

This is a tart without a crust.

Preheat oven to 350°F.

6   large potatoes
2   cups warm milk
6   tablespoons sweet butter or margarine
8   eggs, 3 beaten and 5 hard-cooked
8   ounces Gruyère or Swiss cheese, shredded
2   tablespoons chopped fresh parsley
1   cup chopped hazelnuts
½   teaspoon salt
½   teaspoon white pepper
¼   teaspoon nutmeg
    oil
½   cup wheat germ or unflavored bread crumbs

Wash potatoes and place, unpeeled, in a saucepan of boiling salted water. Bring to a boil; reduce heat, cover, and boil for 40 to 60 minutes, or until potatoes are fork tender. Drain, peel, and put through a potato ricer or food processor, and puree. Transfer to a mixing bowl; add warm milk, 2 tablespoons butter, and 3 beaten eggs. Mix well.

Add shredded cheese, parsley, hazelnuts, salt, pepper, and nutmeg; mix until well blended and smooth.

Sprinkle a well-oiled spring-form cake pan with 2 tablespoons wheat germ; spoon half of the potato mixture into pan. Slice hard-cooked eggs and arrange on top of potatoes; spoon in remaining half of potato mixture; sprinkle with remaining wheat germ and dot with remaining butter.

Bake for 20 to 30 minutes, or until a golden crust has formed. Set aside for a few minutes before removing from pan. Serve hot. Serves 6.

SPINACH TART
Crostata di spinaci

Preheat oven to 400°F.

1 recipe for pastry (see recipe for Artichoke Tart earlier in this chapter), less 1 tablespoon water
2 pounds fresh spinach, or
20 ounces frozen spinach leaves, thawed and drained
3 tablespoons sweet butter or margarine
1 small onion, chopped
1 clove garlic, minced
6 slices bacon, diced
½ cup grated Parmesan or Asiago cheese
½ teaspoon salt
3 eggs, slightly beaten

Prepare pastry.

To prepare filling, remove roots and hard stems from spinach; wash in several changes of water. Place spinach in vegetable steamer with 1 inch salted water. Cover and steam for 5 minutes. Drain and squeeze out any excess water.

Melt butter in a saucepan; add onion and garlic, and cook until onion is tender; add diced bacon and cook until crisp. Add spinach, cheese, salt and eggs; cook, stirring, for 5 minutes. Spoon filling into baked shell.

Proceed as in Artichoke Tart recipe. Bake for 15 to 20 minutes, or until nicely golden. Serves 6.

SQUASH TART
Crostata di zucca

This *crostata* is for that special occasion when you want to forget everything about calories.

Preheat oven to 400°F.
Pastry:
- 1 cup flour
- 6 tablespoons sweet butter or margarine, at room temperature
- ¼ teaspoon salt
- 2 eggs
  pinch white pepper
  pinch nutmeg
  butter and flour for baking pan

Filling:
- 4 eggs
- 2½ pounds Hubbard squash, cooked and mashed
- 1½ cups light cream
- 6 tablespoons Amaretto liqueur
- 1 teaspoon cinnamon
- 2 teaspoons grated fresh lemon rind
- ½ teaspoon salt
- 1 teaspoon almond extract

To prepare pastry, follow recipe for Asparagus Tart earlier in this chapter, using above ingredients.

To prepare filling, in a mixing bowl beat eggs with mashed squash; add cream, Amaretto, cinnamon, lemon rind, salt, and almond extract. Beat until smooth.

Pour into prepared shell. Bake in 425°F oven for 10 minutes; reduce heat to 300°F and bake for 40 minutes, or until knife inserted in center comes out clean. Cool before serving. Serves 6

MOLDS
Sformati

**GREEN OR WAX
BEAN MOLD**

Sformato di fagiolini

Preheat oven to 325°F.
2   pounds fresh green or wax beans, or
20 ounces frozen cut green beans, defrosted
2   tablespoons sweet butter
1   tablespoon grated onion
2   tablespoons flour
1   cup milk
¼   teaspoon salt
¼   teaspoon white pepper
⅛   teaspoon nutmeg
½   cup grated Gruyère or Swiss cheese
6   eggs, separated
    oil

Remove ends from beans. Place beans in vegetable steamer over 1 inch salted water. Cover and steam for 10 minutes. Drain. Transfer to container of an electric blender or food processor; puree thoroughly. Add egg yolks; mix and set aside.

To make sauce, melt butter in a small saucepan over low heat. Add onion and sauté for a few minutes. Add flour, stirring constantly until blended.

In another saucepan scald milk. Pour all at once into butter-flour mixture and stir until thickened. Stir in salt, pepper, and nutmeg; simmer slowly, stirring constantly for 10 minutes. Remove from heat; add grated cheese; stir until melted.

In a bowl combine bean puree with sauce; stir well with a wooden spoon. Beat egg whites until stiff and gently fold into bean mixture. Pour into a well-oiled 8-inch ring mold and set the mold in a pan with 2 inches hot water. Bake for 1 hour. Before serving, invert mold onto a warm serving dish. Serve immediately. Serves 6.

BEET MOLD WITH MUSHROOMS

Sformato di barbabietole con funghi

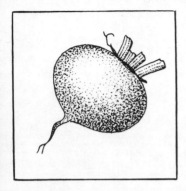

An unusual combination; this complements a lamb dish.

Preheat oven to 375°F.

 2 pounds fresh beets, or
36 ounces whole canned beets, drained
 3 tablespoons sweet butter or margarine
 3 tablespoons corn oil
 1 pound fresh mushrooms, thinly sliced
 2 cloves garlic, minced
½ cup plain yogurt
½ teaspoon salt
½ teaspoon black pepper
 3 eggs, slightly beaten
   oil
 4 tablespoons wheat germ

Wash unpeeled beets, place in vegetable steamer with 1 inch salted water, and steam for 15 minutes. Drain, cool, and peel. Coarsely chop with blender or food processor.

Melt butter in skillet; add oil, sliced mushrooms, and garlic; sauté for 5 minutes. Add chopped beets, stir and sauté 5 more minutes. Remove from heat; stir in yogurt, salt, pepper, and beaten eggs. Mix well. Turn mixture into a well-oiled mold sprinkled with 2 tablespoons wheat germ. Use remaining 2 tablespoons wheat germ to sprinkle on top of mold.

Cover mold with foil; set mold in pan with 2 inches of hot water; bake for 30 minutes. Unmold in warm serving dish and serve. Serves 6.

BROCCOLI MOLD
Sformato di broccoli

Can be prepared ahead of time and baked at the last minute.

Preheat oven to 375°F.

  1 large bunch fresh broccoli, about 3 pounds, or
 40 ounces frozen chopped broccoli, defrosted
  4 eggs, separated
  1 cup shredded Fontina or Fontinella cheese
 ½ teaspoon black pepper
     salt
     butter

Discard outer leaves of broccoli; cut off the lower part of stalks (saving them for a soup). Wash and place in vegetable steamer over 1 inch of salted water. Steam for 6 minutes. Drain well and chop.

Transfer to a large mixing bowl, add egg yolks, shredded cheese, pepper, taste for salt and mix well. Beat egg white until stiff, fold gently into mixture. Spoon mixture into a well-buttered mold; set mold in a pan with 2 inches hot water.

Bake for 20 minutes, or until set. Unmold onto a warm serving dish and serve. Serves 6.

CABBAGE AND COTECHINO MOLD
Sformato di cavolo con cotechino

Cotechino is an Italian sausage that gets its name from "cotenna," meaning pork rind, which is mixed with the pork meat in the sausage. It is available in Italian meat markets.

Preheat oven to 375°F.

  1 cotechino, about 1 pound
  1 medium cabbage, about 3 pounds
 ½ cup Béchamel sauce (see recipe in Chapter 5, Sauces)
  4 eggs, separated
     salt
     pepper
     butter

To prepare cotechino, in a small kettle cover cotechino with cold water and soak for 1 hour. Prick with a fork. Add more water to kettle and bring to a boil. Lower heat; cover and simmer for 3 hours. Leave cotechino in its water until you are ready to use it.

Remove and discard outer leaves of cabbage; core and shred very thin; you may use a food processor. Rinse shredded cabbage well in cold water. Drain and place in a large mixing bowl.

Prepare Béchamel sauce.

Peel cotechino and crumble 2 cups of its meat (you may use remaining sausage for sandwiches, hot or cold). Add meat to cabbage; stir in Béchamel sauce and egg yolks; mix well. Taste for additional salt and pepper.

In another bowl beat egg whites until stiff; fold gently into cabbage mixture. Turn mixture into a well-buttered mold; set mold in a pan with 2 inches hot water. Bake for 20 minutes, or until set. Unmold onto a warm serving dish and serve. Serves 6.

CARDOON MOLD
Sformato di cardi

With this recipe the cardoon will have the crunchy texture of a deep-fried cardoon, but not the calories.

Preheat oven to 350°F.

2½ pounds fresh cardoons
6 eggs
1 cup flour
1 cup unflavored bread crumbs
  oil
1 cup light cream, or
1 cup low-fat yogurt plus 2 tablespoons dry skim milk powder
2 chicken bouillon cubes, crushed
2 lemons

To prepare cardoons, see recipe for Cardoon with Cotechino, Chapter 6. Remove from steamer and drain well.

Beat 2 of the eggs well. Dip each piece of cardoon into flour;

shake off any excess; dip into beaten eggs, then into bread crumbs. Shake off any excess.

Place cardoons in a shallow baking pan. Broil 5 to 7 inches from heat for 3 to 5 minutes; turn pieces and continue to broil for 3 to 5 minutes, or until golden on both sides. Transfer broiled cardoons to a well-oiled square or oblong mold.

In a small bowl combine cream, 4 remaining egg yolks, and crushed bouillon cubes; mix well. Slowly stir in the juice from 1 lemon.

In another bowl beat egg whites until stiff; fold into cream mixture. Spoon over cardoons. Set mold into a pan with 2 inches boiling water. Cover mold with aluminum foil. Bake for 30 minutes. Before serving, unmold onto a warm serving dish. Serves 6.

CARROT MOLD
Sformato di carote

Very good with baked ham.

Preheat oven to 375°F.
- 2 pounds fresh carrots, grated
- 4 tablespoons melted sweet butter or margarine
- 2 eggs, separated
- ½ cup wheat germ
- ½ cup grated Gruyère or Swiss cheese
- ½ cup flour
- ½ teaspoon baking soda
- ½ teaspoon salt
- ½ teaspoon white pepper
- butter for mold

In a mixing bowl combine grated carrots, melted butter, egg yolks, wheat germ, grated cheese, flour, baking soda, salt, and pepper. Mix by hand until well blended. Beat egg whites until stiff and gently fold into carrot mixture. Spoon mixture into well-buttered mold and set in a pan with 2 inches hot water. Bake for 30 minutes, or until set. Unmold onto a warm serving dish and serve. Serves 6.

CAULIFLOWER MOLD
Sformato di cavolfiore

Preheat oven to 375°F.
1 cauliflower head, about 2 pounds
3 tablespoons sweet butter or margarine
1 cup Béchamel sauce (see recipe in Chapter 5, Sauces)
½ cup grated Gruyère or Swiss cheese
3 eggs, separated
butter for mold

To prepare cauliflower, see recipe for Cauliflower with Bagna Caôda, Chapter 2. Place cauliflower with butter in container of an electric blender or food processor and blend until pureed.

Prepare Béchamel sauce. Stir in grated cheese and combine with pureed cauliflower in a mixing bowl. Stir in egg yolks one at a time. Beat egg whites until stiff and fold into cauliflower mixture. Spoon mixture into a well-buttered mold and set in a pan with 2 inches hot water. Bake for 40 minutes, or until set. Unmold onto a warm serving dish and serve. Serves 6.

EGGPLANT MOLD
Sformato di melanzane

Preheat oven to 375°F.
3 tablespoons olive oil
2 medium eggplants, about 2 pounds, peeled and cubed
2 medium sweet onions, coarsely chopped
1 clove garlic, minced
1 tablespoon chopped fresh basil
1 tablespoon chopped fresh parsley
1 teaspoon salt
½ teaspoon black pepper
1 cup grated Gruyère or Swiss cheese
4 eggs, separated
butter
4 tablespoons wheat germ

Place oil in a large skillet; add cubed eggplants, onions, and garlic. Sauté over medium heat for 10 minutes, stirring occasionally. Transfer to the container of an electric blender or food processor, and blend until smooth. Cool.

Place pureed eggplant mixture in a mixing bowl; stir in chopped basil and parsley, salt, pepper, grated cheese, and egg yolks one at a time. In a separate bowl, beat egg whites until stiff; fold gently into eggplant mixture. Spoon mixture into a well-buttered mold; sprinkle top with wheat germ.

Set mold in a pan with 2 inches of hot water, and bake for 25 to 30 minutes, or until firm. Gently unmold onto a warm serving dish and serve hot. Serves 6.

FENNEL MOLD
Sformato di finocchi

Preheat oven to 375°F.
6 medium fennels
1 cup Béchamel sauce (see recipe in Chapter 5, Sauces)
½ cup grated Gruyère or Swiss cheese
4 eggs, separated
¼ teaspoon white pepper
salt to taste
butter

To prepare fennels, see recipe for Fennel Frittata, Chapter 7. Drain and transfer to container of electric blender or food processor; cover and process until coarsely chopped.

Prepare Béchamel sauce.

Pour fennels into a mixing bowl. Add sauce, grated cheese, egg yolks one at a time, pepper, and salt to taste; mix well. Beat egg whites until stiff, fold gently into fennel mixture. Spoon mixture into a well-buttered mold; set mold in a baking pan with 2 inches hot water.

Bake for 20 minutes or until set. Unmold onto a warm serving dish and serve. Serves 6.

KALE MOLD
Sformato di cavolo riccio

Preheat oven to 375°F.
2 pounds fresh kale
3 tablespoons sweet butter or margarine
1 cup Béchamel sauce (see recipe in Chapter 5, Sauces)
⅛ teaspoon nutmeg
½ cup grated Parmesan or Asiago cheese
4 eggs, separated
salt to taste
butter for mold

Save tough outer leaves and stalks of kale for soup. Rinse remaining leaves well.

Place kale in vegetable steamer over 1 inch cold water. Cover and steam for 8 minutes. Drain well, squeezing out any excess water. Chop coarsely with blender or food processor.

Melt butter in frying pan. Add kale and sauté over medium high heat for 5 minutes, stirring constantly. Transfer to a mixing bowl and cool.

Prepare Béchamel sauce.

When kale has cooled add Béchamel sauce, nutmeg, and cheese, stirring well to mix. Stir in egg yolks one at a time. Taste for additional salt. Beat egg whites until stiff; fold gently into kale mixture. Spoon mixture into a well-buttered mold; set mold in a pan with 2 inches hot water.

Bake for 45 minutes or until firm. Unmold onto a warm serving dish and serve. Serves 6.

LENTIL MOLD
Sformato di lenticchie

Preheat oven to 375°F.

1½	cups dried lentils, or
20	ounces canned lentils, drained
½	cup barley
1	cup homemade or canned chicken broth
1	teaspoon salt
½	teaspoon white pepper
¼	teaspoon nutmeg
1	cup wheat germ
½	cup shredded Gruyère or Swiss cheese
1	clove garlic, chopped
1	medium onion, finely chopped
1	tablespoon chopped fresh parsley
1	celery stalk, finely chopped
2	eggs, separated
	butter

To prepare lentils, wash and drain. Place them in a saucepan; cover with water and bring to a boil. Cover pan and boil for 2 minutes. Remove from heat and let stand in water for at least 2 hours. Drain.

Meanwhile, place barley in a saucepan with the broth; bring to a boil; reduce heat, cover and simmer over low heat for 40 minutes. Drain if necessary.

Transfer lentils and barley to a large mixing bowl; add salt, pepper, nutmeg, wheat germ, shredded cheese, garlic, onion, parsley, celery, and beaten egg yolks; mix well.

Beat egg whites until stiff; fold gently into lentil mixture. Spoon mixture into well-buttered mold; set mold in a pan with 2 inches hot water.

Bake for 35 minutes, or until set. Let stand 15 minutes before unmolding onto a warm serving dish. Serve hot with your favorite tomato sauce or meat gravy. Serves 6.

MUSHROOM MOLD
Sformato di funghi

Preheat oven to 375°F.
- 3 tablespoons sweet butter or margarine
- 1 small onion, finely chopped
- 2 tablespoons chopped fresh parsley
- 1 pound fresh mushrooms, thinly sliced
- 5 eggs, separated
- ½ cup light cream or yogurt
- ½ cup wheat germ
- ½ cup grated Gruyère or Swiss cheese
  butter for mold

Melt butter in skillet; add onions and sauté until onions are soft. Add parsley and sliced mushrooms and cook for 5 minutes, stirring occasionally. Remove from heat, stir in egg yolks one at a time; add cream, wheat germ (reserve 2 tablespoons for topping), and grated cheese; stir well to mix.

Beat egg whites until stiff; fold gently into mushroom mixture.

Spoon mixture into well-buttered mold; set mold in a pan with

2 inches hot water. Bake for 20 minutes, or until set. Set aside for 10 minutes before unmolding onto a warm serving dish. Serves 6.

MUSHROOM AND POTATO MOLD

Sformato di patate con funghi

For a variation, use one pound of *cotechino*, cooked and crumbled, instead of the mushrooms.

Preheat oven to 400°F.

- 2 pounds baking potatoes
- 1 small onion, chopped
- 1 small clove garlic, minced
- 4 tablespoons corn oil
- 1 pound fresh firm mushrooms, thinly sliced
- 1 beef bouillon cube
- ½ cup dry Marsala or port wine
- 4 tablespoons melted sweet butter or margarine
- ½ cup grated Gruyère or Swiss cheese
- 2 eggs, beaten
- 3 tablespoons flour
  oil for mold

Wash potatoes and put in a saucepan with salted water; bring to a boil; reduce heat, cover, and cook for 30 minutes, or until fork tender. Drain. Peel and put through a potato ricer or food processor and puree. Transfer to a mixing bowl.

While the potatoes are cooking, place chopped onion, garlic, and mushrooms in a frying pan with the oil; sauté until onions are soft. Dissolve beef bouillon cube in wine and add to onion and mushrooms in pan; raise the heat, stir, and cook until the wine has evaporated.

Add melted butter to mashed potatoes; stir in grated cheese, eggs, and flour. Stir in onion-mushroom mixture and blend well.

Spoon contents into a well-oiled mold; set mold in a pan with 2 inches boiling water. Bake for 40 minutes, or until firm. Set aside for 5 minutes before unmolding. Serves 6.

ONION AND POTATO MOLD
Sformato di cipolle con patate

Preheat oven to 350°F.

- 3 tablespoons corn oil
- 2 pounds onions, peeled and thinly sliced
- 1 cup homemade or canned beef broth
- 3 pounds potatoes, peeled, diced, and cooked
- 4 tablespoons sweet butter or margarine
- 1½ cups hot milk
- 4 tablespoons grated Parmesan or Asiago cheese
- 2 eggs, separated
- ½ teaspoon salt
- ½ teaspoon white pepper
- 1 teaspoon dried marjoram
- 4 tablespoons wheat germ
  butter for mold

Heat oil in skillet; add onions and sauté until golden and soft; add broth, cover, and cook over low heat for 15 minutes.

Meanwhile, place mashed potatoes in a saucepan; add butter and stir over low heat, until butter has melted. Add milk; stir until milk is absorbed. Remove from heat; add grated cheese and egg yolks; stir well to mix. Add salt and pepper, stir and taste for additional salt. Beat egg whites until stiff; fold gently into onion mixture. Spoon mixture into a well-buttered mold. Sprinkle with marjoram and wheat germ. Set mold in a pan with 2 inches of hot water. Bake for 40 minutes, or until set. Unmold onto a warm serving dish and serve. Serves 6.

PEA MOLD
Sformato di piselli

Preheat oven to 375°F.

- 3 pounds fresh peas, shelled, or
- 20 ounces frozen peas, thawed
- 8 ounces sliced boiled ham, julienne
- 1½ cups Béchamel sauce (see recipe in Chapter 5, Sauces)
- ½ teaspoon salt
- ½ teaspoon white pepper
- 6 eggs, separated
  butter

If using fresh peas, place in vegetable steamer with 1 inch salted water. Cover and steam for 20 to 25 minutes or until peas are soft. Drain. Transfer to a blender or food processor and puree.

Prepare Béchamel sauce.

In a bowl combine pureed peas, ham, sauce, salt, and pepper. Stir to mix. Add egg yolks one at a time, and stir. Beat egg whites until stiff; gently fold into pea mixture. Spoon mixture into well-buttered mold.

Set mold in a pan with 2 inches hot water. Bake for 35 to 40 minutes, or until set. Unmold onto a warm serving dish and serve hot. Serves 6.

SPAGHETTI SQUASH MOLD

Sformato di zucca "spaghetti"

A marvelous dish to serve with turkey at Thanksgiving.

Preheat oven to 350°F.

- 3 pounds Spaghetti squash, baked
- 2 tablespoons melted sweet butter or margarine
- 1 cup Béchamel sauce (see recipe in Chapter 5, Sauces)
- 3 eggs, separated
- 6 large *amaretti* (Italian macaroons), crushed
- 1 lemon rind, grated
  pinch salt
  pinch white pepper
  pinch nutmeg
- 2 teaspoons almond extract
- ¼ cup Amaretto liqueur
  butter for mold

Wash squash; punch a number of holes in it with a fork, to prevent it from bursting while cooking. Bake for 1½ hours. Cut in half lengthwise; remove seeds and, with a fork, scrape out the "spaghetti"; as you scrape, you will see it come out.

Prepare Béchamel sauce.

Place spaghetti in a mixing bowl; add butter, sauce, egg yolks, amaretti, lemon rind, salt, pepper, nutmeg, almond extract, and Amaretto liqueur; stir well to mix.

Beat egg whites until stiff; fold gently into squash mixture. Spoon mixture into well-buttered mold; set mold in a pan with 2 inches hot water. Bake for 35 to 40 minutes, or until set. Set aside for a few minutes before unmolding. Unmold onto a warm serving dish and serve. Serves 6.

SPINACH AND HAM MOLD

Sformato di spinaci con prosciutto

Serve with green salad.

Preheat oven to 375°F.

 3 pounds fresh spinach, or
30 ounces frozen chopped spinach, thawed and drained
 3 tablespoons sweet butter or margarine
 5 anchovy fillets, chopped
 2 cups Béchamel sauce (see recipe in Chapter 5, Sauces)
 8 ounces cooked ham, chopped
 1 teaspoon marjoram
 4 tablespoons grated Gruyère or Swiss cheese
 6 eggs, separated
   butter for mold

Remove roots and hard stems from spinach; wash well. Place spinach in vegetable steamer with 1 inch salted water. Cover and steam for 5 minutes. Drain and squeeze out any excess water. Chop.

Melt butter in a skillet; add anchovies and stir and cook for 3 minutes, or until anchovies are melted. Add spinach, stir and cook for 5 minutes. Transfer to a mixing bowl.

Make Béchamel sauce. Add sauce to spinach; stir in chopped ham, marjoram, grated cheese, and egg yolks; stir well to mix.

Beat egg whites until stiff; fold gently into spinach mixture. Spoon mixture into a well-buttered mold; set mold in a pan with 2 inches hot water.

Bake for 30 minutes, or until set. Unmold onto a warm serving dish and serve. Serves 6.

SQUASH MOLD
Sformato di zucca

Serve with Thanksgiving meal.

Preheat oven to 375°F.
- 3 pounds Butternut squash or pumpkin
  milk, enough to cover squash in saucepan
- 2 cups Béchamel sauce (see recipe in Chapter 5, Sauces)
- 4 tablespoons melted sweet butter or margarine
- ½ teaspoon salt
- ½ teaspoon white pepper
- ⅛ teaspoon nutmeg
- ½ cup grated Parmesan or Asiago cheese
- 4 eggs, separated
  oil for mold
- ¼ cup wheat germ

Peel, seed, and cut squash into 1-inch cubes. Place in a saucepan and cover with milk. Bring to a boil; reduce heat, cook uncovered until soft. Drain if necessary and transfer to a blender or food processor and puree. Place in a mixing bowl.

Make Béchamel sauce. Add sauce to pureed squash; stir in melted butter, salt, pepper, nutmeg, and cheese; mix well. Add egg yolks one at a time.

Beat egg whites until stiff. Fold gently into squash mixture. Spoon mixture into a well-oiled mold; sprinkle top with wheat germ; set mold in baking pan with 2 inches hot water.

Bake for 45 minutes, or until set. Unmold onto a warm serving dish and serve. Serves 6.

8 Vegetable Side Dishes and Salads

Verdure, insalate

VEGETABLE SIDE DISHES
Verdure

ARTICHOKES WITH PEAS AND LETTUCE

Carciofi con piselli e insalata

May be served as an accompaniment to chicken or boiled/steamed rice.

6	medium artichokes
1	lemon
2	tablespoons sweet butter or margarine
1	small onion, chopped
4	ounces baked ham, cut into ¼-inch strips
1	teaspoon dried marjoram
½	cup chicken broth, or
½	cup water plus 1 chicken bouillon cube, crumbled
2	pounds fresh peas, shelled, or
1	10-ounce package frozen peas, defrosted, well-drained
½	head Iceberg lettuce, shredded
	salt and pepper to taste

To prepare artichokes, see recipe for Marinated Artichoke Hearts, Chapter 2. Before placing in bowl with lemon juice, cut artichoke into 4 wedges, then cut each wedge into ¼-inch-thick slices, lengthwise.

Melt butter in a large skillet, add onion; cook, stirring for 5 minutes. Add ham; cook for 3 minutes. Drain artichokes well, add to onion and ham mixture in skillet; sprinkle with marjoram and add broth. Cover and simmer for 15 minutes. Add peas and lettuce, simmer 5 minutes longer. Taste for salt and pepper. Serves 6.

ARTICHOKES SWEET AND SOUR

Carciofi in agrodolce

Very good with lamb.

6	large artichokes, or
30	ounces frozen or canned artichoke hearts
2	lemons, 1 sliced
3	cloves garlic
1	small onion
1	small carrot
3	anchovy fillets
10	sprigs fresh parsley
1	teaspoon capers
4	tablespoons corn oil
½	cup dry white wine
2	large tomatoes, or
8	ounces canned chopped plum tomatoes, with their juice
	salt and pepper to taste

To prepare fresh artichokes, see recipe for Marinated Artichoke Hearts, Chapter 2. Before placing in bowl with lemon juice, cut each artichoke into 8 wedges. If using frozen or canned artichoke hearts, defrost and drain; cut into 4 wedges. Set aside.

Place garlic, onion, carrot, anchovies, parsley, and capers in food processor and process until all the vegetables are finely chopped. Heat oil in skillet; add pureed vegetables. Cook for 10 minutes over medium heat, stirring frequently. Add wine, raise the heat and cook, stirring constantly until wine has evaporated. Add drained artichokes, lemon, tomatoes, and their juice. Cover and cook over low heat until artichokes are tender, about 30 minutes. If using frozen or canned artichoke hearts, cook sauce for 20 minutes, add artichoke hearts, cover, and cook 10 minutes longer. Transfer to warm serving dish, and serve hot. Serves 6.

ARTICHOKE AND SPINACH CASSEROLE
Sformato di carciofi e spinaci

Delicious with chicken or lamb.

Preheat oven to 350°F.
- 3 tablespoons sweet butter or margarine
- 3 shallots, chopped
- 8 ounces marinated artichoke hearts, drained and diced
- 2 pounds fresh spinach, cooked, chopped, or
- 20 ounces frozen chopped spinach, defrosted and drained
- ½ teaspoon dried tarragon
- ½ teaspoon dried marjoram
- ½ cup wheat germ
- ½ cup grated Swiss cheese
- 2 eggs, lightly beaten
  butter for casserole

Heat butter in a skillet; add shallots and sauté for 5 minutes. Remove from heat, add artichoke hearts, spinach, tarragon, marjoram, wheat germ, grated cheese, and eggs. Stir to mix well. Transfer to a well-buttered casserole. Bake for 25 minutes. Serves 6.

ARTICHOKES WITH PARSLEY AND GARLIC
Carciofi trifolati

Very tempting with sautéed pork chops.

- 4 large artichokes
- 1 lemon
- 6 tablespoons corn oil
- 2 cloves garlic, chopped
- ½ teaspoon salt
- ½ teaspoon black pepper
- ½ cup chopped fresh parsley

To prepare artichokes, see recipe for Marinated Artichoke Hearts, Chapter 2. Before placing in bowl with lemon juice, cut each artichoke into 8 wedges and cut each wedge lengthwise into ¼-inch-thick slices.

Heat oil in skillet, add garlic; drain artichokes and sauté with the garlic for 5 minutes. Sprinkle with salt, and pepper; lower heat, cover and simmer for 20 minutes. Stir in parsley, cook 5 minutes longer, and serve. Serves 4 to 6.

ARTICHOKES ALLA GIUDEA
Carciofi alla Giudea

An excellent vegetable with roast leg of lamb.

6	small artichokes
1	lemon, sliced
3 or 4	cups oil for frying
3	cloves garlic
	salt and pepper to taste

To prepare artichokes, see recipe for Marinated Artichoke Hearts, Chapter 2. Instead of soaking in bowl, insert a melon ball cutter into the center of each artichoke, twist it to remove the center fuzzy choke without breaking open the artichoke. Rub all the cut surfaces of the artichokes to prevent them from turning brown.

Heat oil in heavy skillet; add garlic, brown it, and remove it from oil. When oil is very hot, add artichokes, top side down, turning to brown on all sides. Continue cooking and turning until artichokes are tender, about 10 minutes. Drain on paper towels, sprinkle with salt and pepper to taste; serve hot. Serves 6.

SAUTÉED ASPARAGUS
Asparagi fritti

Good with any meats or as a hot appetizer.

3	pounds fresh asparagus, or
30	ounces frozen or canned asparagus spears, defrosted and well drained
½	cup flour
2	eggs, beaten
1	cup unflavored breadcrumbs
4	tablespoons grated Parmesan or Asiago cheese
3	tablespoons sweet butter or margarine
3	tablespoons corn oil
1	teaspoon salt
¼	teaspoon white pepper

To prepare fresh asparagus, see recipe for Asparagus and Prosciutto Rolls, Chapter 2.

Dip each spear into flour, then into eggs, and then into bread crumbs combined with grated cheese. Melt butter in a frying pan; add oil and sauté asparagus for 5 minutes, or until nicely browned all around. Transfer to a warm serving dish; sprinkle with salt and pepper and serve hot. Serves 6.

ASPARAGUS WITH ANCHOVY SAUCE
Asparagi all'acciuga

Good accompaniment to broiled fish fillets.

36	fresh asparagus, or
36	frozen or canned asparagus spears, defrosted and well drained
6	tablespoons sweet butter or margarine
6	anchovy fillets, finely chopped
	juice of 1 lemon
½	teaspoon white pepper

To prepare fresh asparagus, see recipe for Asparagus and Prosciutto Rolls, Chapter 2. Remove from heat, but leave asparagus in steamer to keep warm.

Meanwhile, melt butter in a small saucepan over low heat; add chopped anchovies and cook until anchovies have melted. Add the lemon juice; stir and cook over very low heat for 5 minutes.

Drain asparagus well. Arrange in a warm serving dish with all the tips on one side of dish; pour sauce over tips; sprinkle with pepper and serve warm. Serves 6.

ASPARAGUS WITH BUTTER CHEESE
Asparagi al burro e formaggio

Delicious with sautéed baby lamb chops.

2 pounds fresh asparagus, or
20 ounces frozen or canned asparagus spears, defrosted, and well drained
6 tablespoons melted sweet butter or margarine
½ cup grated Parmesan or Asiago cheese

To prepare fresh asparagus, see recipe for Asparagus and Prosciutto Rolls, Chapter 2.

Arrange asparagus with tips all on one side on a warm serving dish. Pour hot melted butter over and sprinkle with cheese. Serves 4 to 6.

ASPARAGUS WITH MUSTARD SAUCE
Asparagi con salsa alla senape

Good with pork entrée.

36 fresh asparagus, or
36 frozen or canned asparagus spears, defrosted and well drained
2 teaspoons prepared mustard
3 tablespoons chopped fresh parsley
½ cup olive oil
salt to taste

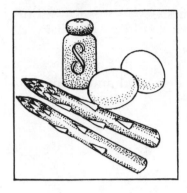

To prepare fresh asparagus, see recipe for Asparagus and Prosciutto Rolls, Chapter 2. Drain well and cool.

In a small bowl combine mustard, parsley, and oil; beat with wire whisk for 2 minutes; taste for salt.

Arrange asparagus in serving dish with tips all on one side of dish. Pour sauce over asparagus tips and keep at room temperature until serving time. It may be prepared up to 2 hours before serving. Serves 6.

CRANBERRY BEANS WITH RED WINE
Fagioli burlotti al Barbera

A good accompaniment to any wild game dish.

2   cups dried cranberry beans
2   cups Barbera wine or any dry red wine of your choice
1   small onion, coarsely chopped
1   whole large potato, peeled
8   ounces cooked ham, diced
4   whole cloves
1   teaspoon rosemary leaves
½   teaspoon black pepper
3   tablespoons olive oil
1   teaspoon salt

Wash dried beans. Soak in enough water to cover beans, overnight, or boil beans for 3 minutes; remove from heat; cover pot and let stand for 2 hours. Drain. Place soaked beans in a large pot with wine; add enough water to cover beans. Add onion, potato, ham, cloves, rosemary, pepper, and oil. Bring to a boil, reduce heat, cover pot, and simmer for 1½ hours, or until beans are tender.

Add salt, stir, transfer to a warm serving dish. Serves 6 to 8.

FRIED GREEN OR WAX BEANS
Fagiolini fritti

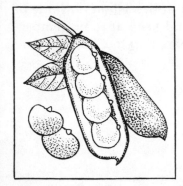

An easy and quick way to prepare beans.

2 pounds fresh green or wax beans, or
20 ounces frozen whole green beans, defrosted and drained
4 tablespoons corn oil
2 cloves garlic, thinly sliced
1 medium onion, thinly sliced
1 green pepper, diced
¼ cup dry white wine
½ teaspoon salt
½ teaspoon black pepper
2 tablespoons chopped fresh basil or parsley

Remove ends and strings from fresh beans. Place in vegetable steamer with 1 inch salted water. Cover and steam for 7 minutes; drain.

Heat oil in a large skillet; add garlic, onion, and green pepper. Stir and cook for 5 minutes; add beans, wine, salt, and pepper. Simmer uncovered for 10 minutes. Raise the heat and stir and cook for 2 minutes, or until the wine has evaporated. Add basil, stir, taste for additional salt and pepper, and serve hot. Serves 6.

GREEN OR WAX BEANS WITH ANCHOVIES
Fagiolini con acciughe

An unusual combination that goes well with pork.

2 pound fresh green or wax beans, or
20 ounces frozen whole green beans, defrosted and drained
2 tablespoons olive oil
2 tablespoons sweet butter
2 tablespoons chopped fresh chives
1 small clove garlic, minced
4 anchovy fillets, chopped
½ teaspoon black pepper
  salt to taste

To steam beans see preceding recipe for Fried Green or Waxed Beans.

Heat oil in a skillet; add butter, chopped chives, garlic, anchovies, and pepper. Sauté for 3 minutes; add green beans and cook uncovered over medium heat for 10 minutes, stirring occasionally. Taste for salt, and serve hot. Serves 6.

GREEN OR WAX BEANS WITH MUSTARD SAUCE
Fagiolini alla mostarda

Very good accompaniment to baked ham.

2	pounds fresh green or wax beans, or
20	ounces frozen green beans, defrosted and drained
3	tablespoons sweet butter or margarine
3	teaspoons prepared mustard
½	teaspoon salt
¼	teaspoon white pepper
4	tablespoons wheat germ

To steam beans see recipe for Fried Green or Wax Beans earlier in this chapter. Cut into 2-inch pieces before steaming. Remove from heat but leave in steamer to keep warm.

In a small saucepan melt butter; stir in mustard, salt, and pepper. Stir over low heat for 2 minutes.

Drain beans, transfer to a warm serving bowl; pour mustard sauce and wheat germ over beans; toss gently, and taste for additional salt and pepper. Serve hot. Serves 6.

GREEN OR WAX BEANS WITH ANISE SEEDS
Fagiolini con semi di finocchio

An unusual flavor; goes well with fish.

2	pounds fresh green or wax beans, or
20	ounces frozen whole green beans, defrosted and drained
4	tablespoons olive oil
1	large onion, thinly sliced
½	teaspoon salt
¼	teaspoon black pepper
1	teaspoon crushed anise seeds
1	tablespoon tomato paste with 2 tablespoons hot water

To steam beans see recipe for Fried Green or Wax Beans earlier in this chapter.

Heat oil in a skillet; add onion and cook for 5 minutes over medium heat. Add green beans, sprinkle with salt, pepper, and crushed anise seed. Cook for 5 minutes, stirring occasionally. Mix tomato paste with hot water and pour over beans; stir. Cover and cook over low heat for 10 minutes. Place in serving bowl and serve. Serves 6.

SWEET AND SOUR GREEN OR WAX BEANS
Fagiolini in salsa agrodolce

Delicious with broiled chicken.

2 pounds fresh green or wax beans, or
20 ounces frozen green beans, defrosted and well drained
2 tablespoons brown sugar or honey
¼ cup wine vinegar
2 egg yolks
¼ cup water

To prepare beans see recipe for Fried Green or Wax Beans earlier in this chapter. Keep warm.

In a small saucepan, combine sugar, vinegar, egg yolks, and water; cook over low heat, stirring constantly, until sauce is thickened and smooth. *Do not boil* or sauce will curdle.

Transfer beans to a warm serving dish; pour sauce over and serve hot. Serves 6.

ITALIAN GREEN BEANS WITH SCALLIONS
Taccole con cipollotti

4 tablespoons sweet butter or margarine
3 bunches scallions, sliced, white parts plus two inches of the green
20 ounces frozen Italian green beans
½ teaspoon salt
¼ teaspoon white pepper
2 tablespoons tarragon vinegar or white vinegar
½ cup chopped fresh parsley

Melt butter in a skillet; add sliced scallions and cook for 5 minutes or until scallions are soft.

Meanwhile, cook beans according to package directions; drain well. Add to scallions in skillet; sprinkle with salt and pepper; stir and cook over medium heat for 5 minutes. Sprinkle with vinegar and parsley; stir and cook 5 minutes longer. Serve hot. Serves 6.

BAKED LIMA BEANS PEASANT-STYLE
Fagioli di Spagna alla contadina

A good change from baked beans.

Preheat oven to 350°F.
  2 cups dried large lima beans, or
 22 ounces canned lima beans, drained
  1 16-ounce can chopped Italian plum tomatoes, with their juice
  2 tablespoons chopped fresh basil, or
  2 teaspoons dried basil
  1 teaspoon dried marjoram
  1 large clove garlic, minced
  1 medium onion, grated
  1 cup shredded Gruyère or Swiss cheese
 ½ teaspoon salt
 ½ teaspoon black pepper
  1 cup coarsely chopped hazelnuts or walnuts
 ¼ cup wheat germ
     oil for casserole

Wash beans thoroughly. Place beans in a bowl and cover with water. Soak overnight. Or, boil beans for 3 minutes; remove from heat; cover pot and let stand for 2 hours. Drain.

Transfer soaked beans to a saucepan. Cover with hot water plus 2 inches. Cover pan; bring to a boil; reduce heat and cook for 1½ to 2 hours, or until beans are tender. Drain.

Place soaked beans in a large mixing bowl; add chopped tomatoes, with their juice, basil, marjoram, garlic, onion, shredded cheese, salt, pepper, and nuts. Mix well.

Transfer to a greased bake-and-serve casserole; sprinkle wheat germ on top of bean mixture. Bake for 35 minutes. Serves 6.

BEETS WITH BÉCHAMEL SAUCE

Barbabietole con Besciamella

Preheat broiler.

2   pounds fresh beets, or
32 ounces canned sliced beets, drained
2   cups Béchamel sauce (see recipe in Chapter 5, Sauces)
4   tablespoons butter or margarine

Wash fresh unpeeled beets; place in vegetable steamer over 1 inch salted water, and steam for 15 minutes. Drain, peel, and cut into ¼-inch-thick slices.

Prepare Béchamel sauce; set aside.

Melt butter in a saucepan over medium heat; add sliced beets; stir and cook for 5 minutes. Transfer to a bake-and-serve dish; pour sauce over beets. Broil for a few minutes; do not let it get golden, just hot. Serves 6.

SAUTÉED BELGIAN ENDIVES

Indivia Belga in padella

6   large heads Belgian endive
½   cup olive oil
2   cloves garlic, peeled and mashed
4   anchovy fillets, minced
½   teaspoon white pepper
2   tablespoons chopped fresh chives

Remove any discolored outer leaves from endives; cut into ½-inch-thick slices (you will have rings). Rinse in cold water and drain well.

Heat oil in a skillet; add garlic and sauté until golden. Discard garlic. Add minced anchovies to oil in skillet; stir and cook over medium heat for 2 minutes. Add endive to anchovies, cover, and cook for 20 minutes, stirring occasionally. Add chives and pepper; stir and cook 10 minutes longer. Serves 6.

BROCCOLI CASSEROLE
Broccoli al forno

Preheat oven to 350°F.

1 large bunch fresh broccoli, about 3 pounds, or
40 ounces frozen chopped broccoli, defrosted and drained
 oil for baking pan
1 cup soft bread crumbs
5 tablespoons melted sweet butter or margarine
2 hard-cooked eggs, chopped
½ teaspoon salt
¼ teaspoon white pepper
1 tablespoon fresh lemon juice
1 teaspoon sweet paprika

Discard outer leaves of broccoli. Cut off lower part of stems. Place in vegetable steamer with 1 inch salted water and steam for 6 minutes. Chop. Transfer broccoli to a well-oiled bake-and-serve dish. Set aside.

In a small bowl combine bread crumbs, melted butter, chopped eggs, salt, pepper, and lemon juice. Mix well. Spread mixture over broccoli and sprinkle with paprika. Bake for 15 minutes. Serve hot. Serves 6.

SAUTÉED BROCCOLI WITH SOYBEAN SPROUTS
Broccoli saltati con germogli di soia

The perfect choice for a vegetarian meal.

3 tablespoons corn oil
2 medium carrots, cut into thin strips
1 large onion
1 bunch broccoli, about 1 pound, diced
8 ounces soybean sprouts
½ teaspoon salt
1 teaspoon dried tarragon
4 ounces fresh mushrooms, sliced

Heat oil in a large skillet; add carrots, onion, broccoli, and sprouts; cook and stir over high heat for 4 minutes. Add salt, tarragon, and mushrooms. Reduce heat; cover and cook 5 minutes longer, stirring occasionally. Serves 6.

SAUTÉED BRUSSELS SPROUTS
Cavolini di Bruxelles in padella

2 pounds fresh brussels sprouts, or
20 ounces frozen brussels sprouts, defrosted, drained
4 tablespoons corn oil
2 large onions, thinly sliced
1 teaspoon salt
¼ teaspoon black pepper
3 tablespoons chopped fresh parsley
1 teaspoon dried thyme

To prepare brussels sprouts, clean, remove the outer wilted leaves, cut off stems, and cut a small cross on bottom of each. Place in vegetable steamer with 1 inch salted water and steam for 12 to 14 minutes. Drain.

Heat oil in skillet, add onions and sauté over medium heat until soft; add sprouts, salt, pepper, parsley, and thyme. Stir and cook for 5 minutes. Transfer to a warm serving dish and serve. Serves 6.

BRUSSELS SPROUTS WITH HAM
Cavolini di Bruxelles con prosciutto

Preheat oven to 350°F.
1½ pounds fresh brussels sprouts, or
20 ounces frozen brussels sprouts, defrosted, drained
2 cups Béchamel sauce (see recipe in Chapter 5, Sauces)
8 ounces plum tomatoes, drained and chopped
8 ounces baked ham, thinly sliced
oil for baking pan
½ cup grated Gruyère or Swiss cheese

To prepare brussels sprouts, see preceding recipe for Sautéed Brussels Sprouts.

Prepare Béchamel sauce.

Place sprouts with Béchamel sauce, tomatoes, and ham, in alternating layers in a well-oiled bake-and-serve dish. End with sauce and sprinkle with the grated cheese. Bake for 10 minutes. Serves 6.

BRAISED CABBAGE WITH BACON

Cavolo cappuccino brasato con pancetta

Pancetta is the Italian name for the same cut as bacon, but it is never smoked. It is not easily available, but you can use smoked bacon; it works very well in many recipes.

1   medium cabbage, shredded (you may use a food processor for shredding)
8   ounces lean bacon
4   medium carrots, diced
2   medium whole onions, peeled
3   whole cloves
1   teaspoon dried thyme
3   bay leaves
½   cup dry white wine
    salt and pepper to taste

Remove and discard outer leaves of cabbage. Core, shred, and rinse well in cold water. Place in vegetable steamer with 1 inch salted water, and steam for 10 minutes. Drain.

Arrange half of bacon slices in bottom of a saucepan; add carrots, onions, cloves, thyme; and bay leaves. Cook over medium heat for 5 minutes. Add cabbage and wine. Stir well. Taste for salt and pepper. Cook for 20 minutes, stirring occasionally. Serve hot. Serves 6.

CARDOON IN TOMATO SAUCE

Cardi al pomodoro

Serve with boiled or steamed rice.

2½   pounds fresh cardoons
2   lemons
½   teaspoon salt
1   teaspoon dried marjoram
4   tablespoons corn oil
1   medium onion, chopped
1   clove garlic, minced
¼   cup dry white wine
8   ounces homemade (for recipe see Chapter 5) or commercial tomato sauce

To prepare cardoons, see recipe for Cardoon with Cotechino, Chapter 6. Transfer to a large shallow dish, sprinkle with the juice of the remaining lemon, salt, and marjoram; stir and set aside.

Heat oil in a saucepan; sauté onions and garlic for 5 minutes; add wine and cook 5 minutes longer. Add tomato sauce and cardoons; stir. Cook over medium heat for 10 minutes. Transfer to a warm serving dish and serve. Serves 6.

BAKED CARDOON WITH BÉCHAMEL SAUCE
Cardi al forno con Besciamella

Very good for a change, with pork and lamb.

Preheat oven to 350°F.

2½ pounds fresh cardoons
  4 tablespoons sweet butter or margarine
     oil for casserole
  2 cups Béchamel sauce (see recipe in Chapter 5, Sauces)
  ½ cup shredded Fontina or Fontinella cheese
  3 egg yolks

To prepare cardoons, see recipe for Cardoon with Cotechino, Chapter 6.

Melt butter in large skillet; add cardoons and gently sauté for 5 minutes. Transfer to a well-oiled bake-and-serve casserole.

Make Béchamel sauce; remove from heat. Add grated cheese and stir until cheese has melted. Add egg yolks one at a time, stirring after each addition. Pour sauce over cardoons, and bake for 15 minutes. Serves 6.

BAKED CARROTS WITH LEMON
Carote al limone

Good accompaniment to fish or fowl, and very low in calories, too.

Preheat oven to 350°F.
- 2 pounds fresh carrots
- ½ teaspoon salt
- ½ teaspoon nutmeg
- ½ cup fresh lemon juice
- 2 tablespoons chopped fresh chives
- oil for casserole

Scrape carrots, wash and cut into 1-inch-thick pieces. Place in bowl and add salt, nutmeg, lemon juice, and chopped chives; mix well. Pour mixture into a greased bake-and-serve casserole.

Cover casserole and bake for 1 hour or until carrots are fork tender. Serves 6.

CARROTS WITH CINNAMON
Carote con canella

- 1½ pounds fresh carrots, or
- 20 ounces frozen cut carrots, defrosted
- 1 cup homemade or canned chicken broth
- 2 tablespoons sweet butter or margarine
- ½ teaspoon rosemary leaves
- 1 teaspoon cinnamon
- ¼ cup tawny port wine
- salt to taste

Scrape fresh carrots and cut into ¼-inch-thick slices. Rinse and place in a saucepan with broth. Bring to a boil, reduce heat, and simmer, uncovered, for 10 minutes.

Melt butter in skillet; add drained carrots, rosemary, and a sprinkle of the cinnamon; sauté for 5 minutes. Add wine; stir and cook until wine has evaporated. Taste for salt. Transfer to a warm serving dish and serve. Serves 6.

**PAN-FRIED
CAULIFLOWER**
Cavolfiore in padella

3 tablespoons corn oil
1 head cauliflower, about 1½ pounds
1 clove garlic, mashed
½ cup dry white wine
½ teaspoon marjoram
½ teaspoon dried basil

To prepare cauliflower, see recipe for Cauliflower with Bagna Caôda, Chapter 2.

Heat oil in frying pan. Add diced cauliflower and garlic; sauté, stirring, for 5 minutes. Add wine, marjoram, and basil; sauté until wine has evaporated. Cauliflower should be crisp, but tender. Discard garlic and transfer cauliflower to a warm serving dish and serve hot. Serves 6.

**BAKED CELERY
WITH MEAT
SAUCE**
*Sedani con sugo di
carne*

Preheat oven to 400°F.
6 cups celery stalks, sliced into 2-inch pieces
  butter for baking pan
2 cups Italian meat sauce (see recipe in Chapter 5, Sauces)
½ cup grated Gruyère or Swiss cheese

Place cut celery in vegetable steamer with 1 inch salted water. Cover and steam for 10 minutes. Drain and transfer to a buttered bake-and-serve dish.

Prepare meat sauce.

Pour sauce over celery; sprinkle with grated cheese. Bake for 15 minutes. Serve hot. Serves 6.

CELERY PATTIES
Polpettine di sedano

4 cups celery stalks, sliced crosswise
3 eggs, beaten
½ teaspoon salt
½ teaspoon white pepper
2 tablespoons chopped fresh parsley
6 tablespoons unflavored bread crumbs or wheat germ
  oil enough for deep frying

Place cut celery in vegetable steamer with 1 inch salted water. Cover and steam for 15 minutes, or until tender. Drain. Transfer to the container of an electric blender or food processor, and puree.

Place pureed celery in a mixing bowl; add beaten eggs, salt, pepper, parsley, and bread crumbs. Mix well.

Heat oil in deep frying pan and drop celery mixture by the spoonful and fry for 2 to 3 minutes, or until golden on all sides. Transfer to paper towels to drain off any fat. Serve hot. Serves 6.

CELERY ROOT OR CELERIAC WITH HAM
Sedano rapa con prosciutto

4   pounds celery roots, peeled and diced
6   tablespoons sweet butter or margarine
1½ cups skim milk plus 3 tablespoons nonfat dry milk powder
1   cup grated Gruyère or Swiss cheese
1   cup diced baked ham
1   teaspoon white pepper
2   tablespoons chopped fresh chives

Place diced celery roots in vegetable steamer with 1 inch salted water. Cover and steam for 15 minutes. Drain well.

Melt butter in a skillet; add milk, combined with milk powder; stir in grated cheese until melted. Add celery roots and diced ham, pepper, and chives; stir and cook over low heat for 5 minutes. Transfer to a warm serving dish and serve. Serves 6.

CELERY ROOTS WITH TARRAGON SAUCE
Sedano rapa al dragoncello

3   pounds celery roots
2   cups homemade or canned chicken broth
4   teaspoons crumbled tarragon leaves
2   teaspoons arrowroot
3   tablespoons melted butter
½   teaspoon white pepper
1   cup dry white wine
    salt to taste

Peel celery roots and cut into match-stick strips. Place in a saucepan with broth and tarragon. Bring to a boil. Reduce heat, cover, and simmer for 15 minutes. Drain and set aside. Reserve liquid.

Combine arrowroot with melted butter and pepper; mix well. Stir into the remaining liquid in saucepan. Add wine, bring to a boil, and boil for 2 or 3 minutes, or until sauce begins to thicken. Return celery roots to sauce, and warm up over low heat. Taste for salt and serve. Serves 6.

SAUTÉED CUCUMBERS
Cetrioli in padella

12	small cucumbers
½	cup flour
½	teaspoon salt
¼	teaspoon white pepper
4	tablespoons sweet butter or margarine
4	tablespoons corn oil

Cut cucumbers into 4 spears each, lengthwise; remove seeds; rinse and drain well.

Combine flour with salt and pepper. Roll each cucumber piece in flour; shake off any excess.

Melt butter in a frying pan; add oil. Sauté cucumbers for about 10 minutes, turning them to be sure that they will be golden on all sides. Serve hot. Serves 6.

CUCUMBER WITH BÉCHAMEL SAUCE
Cetrioli con Besciamella

Preheat oven to 400°F.

6	medium cucumbers
2	cups Béchamel sauce (see recipe in Chapter 5, Sauces)
	butter for baking pan
4	tablespoons chopped fresh parsley
½	cup shredded Gruyère or Swiss cheese
4	tablespoons unflavored bread crumbs or wheat germ

Peel cucumbers; remove seeds; dice. Set aside.

Make Béchamel sauce.

Place cucumbers in a well-buttered bake-and-serve dish; sprinkle with chopped parsley; top with sauce. Sprinkle grated cheese and bread crumbs over sauce. Bake for 10 minutes. Serves 6.

BAKED STUFFED CUCUMBERS

Cetrioli ripieni al forno

When your garden is taken over by cucumbers, you may serve this dish to your friends at a picnic; good hot or cold.

Preheat oven to 375°F.

6	large cucumbers
1	cup Béchamel sauce (See recipe in Chapter 5, Sauces)
1½	cups cooked chicken
2	teaspoons capers
3	anchovy fillets
2	hard-cooked eggs
2	scallions, white part only
½	teaspoon white pepper
½	cup wheat germ

Wash cucumbers, cut in half lengthwise. Do not peel. Scoop out the seeds and discard.

Place in container of a blender or food processor chicken, capers, anchovies, eggs, scallions, and pepper. Process until coarsely chopped. Stir mixture into Béchamel sauce. Fill cucumber halves. Sprinkle with wheat germ and place side by side in a shallow baking dish.

Bake for 20 minutes. Gently transfer to a warm serving dish and serve hot. Serves 6.

BAKED FENNELS WITH CHEESE
Finocchi al forno con formaggio

Very good accompaniment to broiled fish.

Preheat oven to 400°F.
- 6 medium fennels
- 6 tablespoons sweet butter or margarine
- ½ teaspoon salt
- ¼ teaspoon white pepper
- 1 cup homemade or canned chicken broth
- ½ cup grated Gruyère or Swiss cheese

To prepare fennels, discard tops and tough outer leaves. Cut fennels into 6 wedges. Rinse well under running water. Place in vegetable steamer with 1 inch salted water. Cover and steam for 20 minutes. Drain.

Transfer to a well-buttered shallow bake-and-serve dish; arrange in one layer; sprinkle with salt and pepper. Pour broth into dish around base of fennels; dot fennels with 5 tablespoons butter and sprinkle with grated cheese. Bake for 20 minutes. Serve hot. Serves 6.

BAKED FENNELS WITH LOW-CALORIE OPTION
Finocchi al forno

If you don't mind omiting the butter from the recipe, you will have a very tasty low-calorie dish.

Preheat oven to 400°F.
- 6 medium fennels
- 2 chicken bouillon cubes
- ½ cup hot water
- 4 tablespoons sweet butter or margarine (optional)
- 3 tablespoons chopped fresh parsley
- ½ cup wheat germ

To prepare fennels, follow preceding recipe for Baked Fennels with Cheese, cutting them into 4 wedges each.

Dissolve bouillon cubes in hot water; pour into dish around base of fennels; dot with butter; sprinkle with parsley and wheat germ. Bake for 15 minutes. Serve hot. Serves 6.

FRIED FENNELS
Finocchi fritti

6 medium fennels
½ cup flour
3 eggs, lightly beaten
1 to 1½ cups unflavored bread crumbs
  sweet butter or margarine, enough for frying
  salt to taste

To prepare fennels, follow recipe for Baked Fennels with Cheese earlier in this chapter, cutting each in half, then into ¼-inch-thick slices. After steaming, pat dry.

Dip each slice into flour; shake off any excess; dip into beaten eggs, then into bread crumbs; shake off any excess.

Melt butter in large skillet and fry slices on both sides until lightly golden. Drain on paper towels. Transfer to a warm serving dish; sprinkle with salt and serve hot. Serves 6.

JERUSALEM ARTICHOKES WITH BÉCHAMEL SAUCE
Topinambur con Besciamella

Preheat oven to 400°F.
2½ pounds fresh and firm artichokes
  butter for baking pan
2 cups Béchamel sauce (see recipe in Chapter 5, Sauces)
½ cup grated Gruyère or Swiss cheese
½ teaspoon white pepper
4 tablespoons chopped fresh parsley

To prepare artichokes, scrape well with a vegetable brush; rinse and place in a vegetable steamer with 1 inch salted water. Cover and steam for 5 minutes. Drain. Cool long enough to handle, then peel them. Cut artichokes into ½-inch-thick slices. Arrange in a well-greased bake-and-serve dish.

Prepare Béchamel sauce. Pour sauce over; sprinkle with the cheese, pepper, and parsley. Bake for 15 minutes. Serve hot. Serves 6.

JERUSALEM ARTICHOKES BAKED WITH YOGURT
Topinambur al forno con yogurt

Preheat oven to 400°F.

2 pounds fresh, firm Jerusalem artichokes
   oil for baking pan
1½ cups plain yogurt
1 tablespoon chopped fresh dill
½ cup grated Swiss cheese

To prepare artichokes, see preceding recipe for Jerusalem Artichokes with Béchamel sauce. When cool, peel and cut into ¼-inch-thick slices.

Transfer artichokes to a well-greased bake-and-serve dish; arrange in layers, alternating with a little yogurt, sprinkled with some dill and some grated cheese. Finish with yogurt, cheese, and dill. Bake for 15 minutes. Serves 6.

BRAISED KALE WITH CARROTS AND BACON
Cavolo riccio brasato

3 pounds fresh kale
8 slices lean bacon
3 medium carrots, diced
1 large onion, sliced
3 cloves
1 teaspoon thyme
3 bay leaves
1 cup homemade or canned chicken broth
   salt to taste

Discard tough outer leaves and stalks from kale; rinse well. Place kale in vegetable steamer over 1 inch salted water. Cover and steam for 5 minutes. Drain.

Place 4 slices bacon on bottom of a heavy saucepan; spread diced carrots and sliced onion on top. Add cloves, thyme, and bay leaves. Arrange well-drained kale on top; put remaining bacon slices on top of kale. Pour broth in saucepan. Cover and simmer over very low heat for 30 minutes. Salt to taste. Serve hot. Serves 6.

KALE WITH TOMATOES

Cavolo riccio con pomodori

The robust taste of kale goes well with pork or duck.

3 pounds fresh kale
3 tablespoons sweet butter or margarine
1 large onion, thinly sliced
1 clove garlic, minced
8 ounces plum tomatoes, drained and chopped
3 tablespoons chopped fresh parsley
2 tablespoons wine vinegar
  salt and pepper to taste

To prepare kale, cut off and discard tough outer leaves and stalks. Cut leaves into bite-size pieces; rinse well in cold water. Place kale in vegetable steamer with 1 inch salted water. Cover and steam for 5 minutes. Drain and set aside.

Melt butter in a skillet; add onion and garlic and cook until onion is soft. Add tomatoes, parsley, and vinegar; cook over medium heat for 5 minutes, stirring occasionally. Add steamed kale; stir well. Taste for salt and pepper. Cover and cook over low heat for 10 minutes, stirring occasionally. Serve hot. Serves 6.

STIR-FRY KALE
Cavolo riccio in
padella

3 pounds fresh kale
4 tablespoons corn oil
3 cloves garlic, minced
½ teaspoon salt
½ teaspoon black pepper

To prepare kale see preceding recipe for Kale with Tomatoes.

Heat oil in skillet; add garlic and sauté for 2 minutes. Add well-squeezed kale; stir and cook over medium-high heat for 5 minutes. Sprinkle with salt and pepper; stir and serve hot. Serves 6.

LENTIL PUREE
Purea di lenticchie

Very good accompaniment to cooked *cotechino*, or boiled sausages.

2 cups dried lentils
4 tablespoons sweet butter or margarine
1 medium onion, chopped
3 egg yolks
1 cup homemade or canned beef broth
½ teaspoon salt
¼ teaspoon white pepper

To prepare lentils, wash and drain. Place in saucepan; cover with water and bring to a boil. Cover pan and boil for 2 minutes. Remove from heat and let stand in water for at least 2 hours. Drain.

Meanwhile, melt butter in skillet; add onion and cook over low heat until onion is soft. Beat egg yolks into broth; add to onion in skillet; stir and cook for 5 minutes. Add lentils, stir and cook for 5 minutes. Transfer lentil mixture to a blender or food processor and puree. Return to skillet and, over low heat, stir and cook until thick. Add salt and pepper. Serve hot. Serves 6.

LENTILS WITH BACON
Lenticchie con pancetta

2 cups dried lentils
8 slices lean bacon, diced
2 cloves garlic, sliced
3 bay leaves, crumbled
2 tablespoons sweet butter or margarine, at room temperature
1 tablespoon flour
1 tablespoon white vinegar
½ teaspoon salt
½ teaspoon white pepper

To prepare lentils, see preceding recipe for Lentil Purée.

Place bacon in skillet; cook over medium heat, until all the fat is rendered; add garlic, bay leaves, and drained lentils; stir. Reduce heat to low; cover and cook for 10 minutes. If necessary add a little hot water from time to time, to prevent lentils from drying. They should be nice and moist.

Make a paste with butter, flour, and vinegar, and a few minutes before serving, stir mixture into lentils. Stir until butter has melted. Taste for salt and pepper and serve. Serves 6.

LENTILS WITH TOMATO SAUCE
Lenticchie in umido con salsa di pomodoro

2 cups dried lentils
16 ounces canned plum tomatoes
1 large onion, thinly sliced
2 cloves garlic
1 large carrot
2 celery stalks
6 sprigs fresh parsley
2 bay leaves, crumbled
4 tablespoons olive oil
1 teaspoon salt
½ teaspoon black pepper

To prepare lentils, see recipe for Lentil Puree earlier in this chapter.

Place tomatoes, onion, garlic, carrot, celery, and parsley in container of a blender or food processor; process until coarsely chopped.

Heat oil in a saucepan; add bay leaves and tomato mixture; cook over medium heat, stirring occasionally, for 15 minutes. Add lentils; stir. Lower heat; sprinkle with salt and pepper; cover and simmer for 10 minutes. If necessary add a little water, to prevent from drying. Serves 6.

BRAISED LETTUCE WITH CARROTS
Lattuga brasata con carote

Very good with roast chicken.

3 medium heads of Iceberg lettuce
4 ounces Italian prosciutto, diced
2 tablespoons corn oil
4 large carrots, diced
1 clove garlic, minced
2 tablespoons chopped fresh parsley
1 teaspoon dried marjoram
2 tablespoons flour
2 cups homemade or canned beef broth
½ teaspoon white pepper
¼ cup dry white wine
  salt to taste

Discard wilted outer leaves from lettuce. Cut each lettuce head into 4 wedges; rinse and drain well.

Place diced prosciutto with oil in a large skillet, and sauté for 2 minutes; add carrots, garlic, parsley, and marjoram; reduce heat and cook for 5 minutes, stirring occasionally. Add quartered lettuce; cook for 10 minutes, stirring and basting with own juices.

Stir flour into the broth, then pour over lettuce; sprinkle with pepper. Cover skillet, and cook over low heat for 30 minutes, or until lettuce is wilted and tender. Transfer to a warm serving dish; return juices to stove; add wine and, over high heat, cook and stir until liquid is reduced to half. Salt to taste. Pour over lettuce and serve hot. Serves 6.

ROMAINE LETTUCE WITH MUSHROOMS CASSEROLE

Lattuga romana con funghi al forno

Preheat oven to 350°F.

- 1 head romaine lettuce, about 2 pounds
- 5 tablespoons sweet butter or margarine
- 1 pound fresh mushrooms, sliced
- ½ cup grated Gruyère or Swiss cheese
- ½ teaspoon salt
- ½ teaspoon white pepper
- 1 teaspoon dried thyme

Wash lettuce; discard the hard ribs from leaves. Shred remaining lettuce. Place in a vegetable steamer with 1 inch salted water. Cover and steam for 5 minutes. Drain, cook, and squeeze out any water.

Transfer lettuce to a well-buttered bake-and-serve casserole; spread sliced mushrooms over lettuce; sprinkle with grated cheese, salt, pepper, and thyme, and dot with 4 tablespoons butter. Cover. Bake for 30 minutes. Serves 6.

BAKED STUFFED ONIONS

Cipolle ripiene alla Piemontese

There probably are more ways of stuffing onions than there are cities in Italy; this is one of my favorite ways.

Preheat oven to 350°F.

- 6 medium onions
- 2 slices soft white bread, crust removed
- ½ cup milk
- 2 hard-cooked egg yolks, crumbled
- 6 *amaretti* (Italian macaroons), crumbled
- 3 tablespoons grated Parmesan or Asiago cheese
- ⅛ teaspoon cloves
- ⅛ teaspoon cinnamon
- ¼ teaspoon white pepper
- ½ teaspoon salt
- 2 whole eggs, beaten
- 4 tablespoons sweet butter or margarine

Peel onions; place in vegetable steamer with 1 inch salted water. Cover and steam for 15 minutes. Drain; cut onions in half; remove cores and gently shape outer leaves to form a cup. Set aside.

Soak bread in milk for a few minutes; squeeze dry, crumble, and place in a bowl. Add hard-cooked egg yolks, amaretti, grated cheese, cloves, cinnamon, pepper, salt, and beaten eggs; mix well. Fill prepared onions; dot with butter. Arrange side by side in a shallow baking dish. Bake for 30 minutes. Serve hot or cool. Serves 6.

BAKED ONIONS WITH BAGNA CAÔDA

Cipolle arrostite con Bagna Caôda

For you, this dish would be a fine appetizer; I could make a whole meal of it.

Preheat oven to 375°F.
18   medium onions
 1   recipe Bagna Caôda (see recipe for Hot Anchovy-Garlic Dip, Chapter 5, Sauces)

Do not peel onions. Place onions on a baking sheet and bake for 1 to 1½ hours, or until onions are tender. Remove from oven; cut a slice from the root end of each onion and squeeze out the onion from skin. With your hands, take the onions apart and place in a serving bowl.

Prepare Bagna Caôda. Pour hot sauce over and set aside in warm place until serving time. Serves 6.

PEPERONATA
Peperonata

Peperonata means lots of peppers.

6 tablespoons corn oil
4 large onions, thinly sliced
10 large green and red peppers
2 cloves garlic, sliced
3 large fresh tomatoes, or
8 ounces canned plum tomatoes, drained and chopped
1 teaspoon salt
½ teaspoon white pepper
1 teaspoon dried marjoram

To prepare peppers, cut in half, lengthwise; remove seeds and pith; cut into 1-inch pieces. Rinse and drain well.

Heat oil in a large skillet; add onions, peppers, and garlic; sauté over medium-high heat for 5 minutes. Reduce heat, cover, and cook for 20 minutes. Add chopped tomatoes, salt, pepper, and marjoram; stir. Cover and cook for 15 minutes longer. Serve hot. Serves 6.

PEPPERS WITH OLIVES
Peperoni con olive

Great served cold for a picnic; good warm, too.

6 large green and red peppers
6 tablespoons corn oil
2 cloves garlic, minced
4 large tomatoes, sliced
2 tablespoons chopped fresh basil, or
1 teaspoon dried basil
1 teaspoon dried marjoram
8 ounces green olives, pitted and sliced
½ teaspoon salt
½ teaspoon black pepper

To prepare peppers, see preceding recipe for Peperonata.

Place peppers in a large skillet with oil and garlic; sauté for 5 minutes. Reduce heat, cover, and cook for 15 minutes. Add tomatoes; stir in basil and marjoram; cook 5 minutes longer. Remove from heat; add olives. Taste for salt and pepper; stir and serve. Serves 6.

POTATOES SAUTÉED WITH TOMATOES
Patate in padella con pomodori

6	medium potatoes
6	tablespoons corn oil
3	cloves garlic, whole and crushed
16	ounces plum tomatoes, drained and chopped
3	tablespoons chopped fresh parsley
½	teaspoon oregano
1	teaspoon salt
½	teaspoon black pepper

Cook potatoes in boiling salted water (with their skins) for 25 to 35 minutes, or until fork tender. Drain, peel, and cut into ½-inch-thick slices.

Heat oil in a skillet; add garlic and sauté until golden; remove and discard garlic. Add chopped tomatoes; reduce heat and cook uncovered for 15 minutes. Stir in parsley, oregano, salt, and pepper. Cook 5 minutes longer. Add potatoes, cover, and simmer for 5 minutes. Transfer to a warm serving bowl; serve. Serves 6.

POTATO AND CARROT FRITTERS
Frittelle di patate e carote

3	medium potatoes
3	large carrots
½	cup grated Parmesan or Asiago cheese
2	tablespoons chopped fresh parsley
½	cup plain yogurt
4	tablespoons flour
3	eggs, beaten
1	teaspoon salt
½	teaspoon white pepper
¼	teaspoon nutmeg
	oil enough for frying

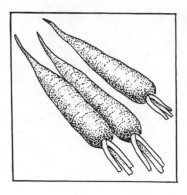

Peel potatoes, and grate; scrape carrots and grate. Place potatoes and carrots in a mixing bowl; add grated cheese, parsley, yogurt, flour, beaten eggs, salt, pepper, and nutmeg; mix well.

Heat oil in frying pan or deep fryer; drop potato mixture by the tablespoonful and cook until golden on all sides. Set on paper towels to dry. Serve hot. Serves 6.

BAKED POTATOES WITH HERBS
Patate aromatiche

If you have an herb garden, by all means use fresh herbs.

Preheat oven to 400°F.
- 6 medium potatoes, peeled and cubed
- 5 tablespoons corn oil
- 5 tablespoons sweet butter or margarine
- ½ teaspoon dried sage leaves
- ½ teaspoon dried rosemary leaves
- 1 tablespoon chopped fresh or frozen chives
- ¼ teaspoon marjoram
- ¼ teaspoon thyme
- 2 tablespoons chopped fresh parsley
- 1 teaspoon salt
- ½ teaspoon black pepper

Place cubed potatoes in a large skillet with oil and butter; sauté, stirring, until golden. Transfer to a baking pan.

In a small bowl combine all the herbs with salt and pepper; mix well. Sprinkle over potatoes; stir to coat well.

Bake for 15 to 20 minutes, or until potatoes are fork tender. Serve hot. Serves 6.

GORGONZOLA CHEESE-STUFFED BAKED POTATOES

Patate ripiene al forno con Gorgonzola

Gorgonzola cheese is the Italian blue cheese.

Preheat oven to 425°F.
- 6 large baking potatoes
- ½ cup light cream or milk
- 4 ounces Gorgonzola cheese, crumbled
- ¼ teaspoon white pepper
- salt to taste
- 2 tablespoons chopped fresh chives

Wash potatoes; dry well. Bake for 40 minutes or until potatoes are fork tender. Cut a slice on top of each potato and scoop out the potato, leaving the skin intact. Mash potato well; add cream, cheese, pepper, salt, and chives. Beat until mixture is fluffy; if necessary, add a little more cream or milk.

Fill skin shell with potato mixture, mounding it slightly. Place potatoes on a baking pan. Bake for a few minutes, or until golden. Serve hot. Serves 6.

SOYBEAN SPROUTS WITH BÉCHAMEL SAUCE

Germogli di soia con Besciamella

Preheat oven to 400°F.
- 1 pound soybean sprouts
- 4 tablespoons corn oil
- 1 clove garlic, peeled and mashed
- 1 beef bouillon cube, crushed
- 1 cup Béchamel sauce (see recipe in Chapter 5, Sauces)
- salt
- 4 tablespoons grated Parmesan or Swiss cheese

Wash sprouts and drop in a saucepan of boiling salted water; cook for 2 minutes; drain well.

Heat oil in a large skillet. Add garlic; cook until garlic has turned brown; discard garlic. Add sprouts and beef cube to oil; stir and cook for 2 minutes. Transfer to a bake-and-serve dish.

Prepare Béchamel sauce and pour over sprouts. Sprinkle grated cheese on top. Bake for 10 minutes. Serves 6.

SWEET POTATO FRITTERS
Fritelle di patate dolci

Preheat oven to 450°F.
6 medium sweet potatoes or yams
2 teaspoons fresh grated lemon rind
½ teaspoon salt
¼ teaspoon nutmeg
½ cup seedless raisins, soaked and drained
3 tablespoons honey (optional)
corn oil enough for frying

Wash potatoes; place in baking pan. Bake for 35 minutes, or until fork tender. Peel; put through a potato ricer or food processor and puree. Transfer to a mixing bowl; add lemon rind, salt, nutmeg, raisins, and honey; mix well.

Heat oil in frying pan or deep fryer; drop potato mixture by the tablespoonful. Cook until golden on all sides. Transfer onto paper towels to dry. Serve hot. Serves 6.

SPINACH WITH PINOLI (PINE NUTS)
Spinaci con pinoli alla romana

Many Italian cookbooks attribute this recipe to the region around Genoa; but according to my friend from Rome, it is actually a Roman specialty.

3 pounds fresh spinach, or
30 ounces frozen spinach leaves, thawed
8 slices thin Italian prosciutto, *pancetta*, or bacon
2 cloves garlic, minced
4 tablespoons sweet butter or margarine
4 tablespoons *pinoli* (pine nuts)
4 tablespoons seedless raisins, soaked and drained

To prepare fresh spinach, trim off roots and hard stems. Wash well in cold water, several times. Place spinach in vegetable steamer with 1 inch salted water. Cover and steam for 5 minutes. Drain and squeeze out any excess water.

Dice prosciutto and place in skillet with garlic; sauté gently until all the fat has been rendered. Add spinach; stir and sauté over medium heat for 5 minutes. Add butter and stir until melted. Stir in pinoli and raisins; transfer to a warm serving bowl and serve. Serves 6.

BAKED SQUASH WITH TOMATOES
Zucca al forno con pomodoro

Preheat oven to 375°F.

  4 pounds summer squash
  4 large fresh ripe tomatoes, peeled and chopped
  1 medium onion, chopped
  6 slices bacon, cooked and crumbled
  2 cups shredded Mozzarella cheese
½ teaspoon salt
½ teaspoon black pepper
  1 teaspoon oregano
     oil for baking pan
½ cup wheat germ
  3 tablespoons sweet butter or margarine

Place unpeeled squash in vegetable steamer with 1 inch salted water. Cover and steam for 20 minutes. Drain, cut in half lengthwise, and remove seeds. Cut into ½-inch-thick slices.

In a bowl, combine tomatoes, onion, bacon, salt, pepper, and oregano; mix well. Place sliced squash in well-oiled baking dish, alternating squash and tomato mixture and cheese. Top with wheat germ, dot with butter. Bake for 30 minutes. Serve hot or cold. Serves 6.

PUREED SQUASH AND POTATOES
Purea di zucca e patate

  2 pounds Butternut squash or pumpkin
  2 large baking potatoes
  4 tablespoons sweet butter or margarine
  2 cups plain yogurt
¼ teaspoon nutmeg
¼ teaspoon white pepper
     salt

To prepare squash, peel, seed, and dice. Place squash in vegetable steamer with 1 inch salted water. Cover and steam for 20 minutes. Drain and mash.

Cook unpeeled potatoes in salted water until soft. Drain, peel, and mash.

Combine in a large saucepan the mashed squash and mashed potatoes; add butter and yogurt; cook and stir over low heat for 10 minutes. Season with nutmeg, pepper, and taste for salt. Serves 6.

SAUTÉED SQUASH
Zucca in padella

½ cup corn oil
3 teaspoons rosemary leaves
3 pounds summer squash, unpeeled and thinly sliced
1 teaspoon salt
½ teaspoon white pepper

Heat oil in frying pan; stir in rosemary and cook for 2 minutes over medium heat. Add sliced squash; sprinkle with salt and pepper. Cook over medium heat, stirring occasionally, for 5 minutes, or until squash is tender but crisp. Transfer to a warm serving dish and serve. Serves 6.

SPAGHETTI SQUASH

The Italian touch with a new vegetable that came from the Orient; most interesting texture, with an excellent taste.

Preheat oven to 350°F.
1 spaghetti squash, about 3 pounds
1 recipe Italian meat sauce (see Chapter 5, Sauces)
grated Parmesan or Asiago cheese

Wash squash; punch holes with a fork in numerous places in the skin, so that it doesn't burst when cooking. Bake for 1½ hours. (Boiling does not work; it gets too soggy.)

Prepare meat sauce.

Cut squash in half lengthwise; remove seeds, then—and here comes the "spaghetti"—scrape the pulp of squash with a fork; you will see all the strings that resemble spaghetti come out. Place it in a warm bowl and serve with meat sauce and grated cheese. Serves 6.

For a change, you can serve it with different sauces, such as: Pesto, Bagna Caôda, homemade Mayonnaise (cold), and Green Sauce (cold). For recipes see Chapter 5, Sauces.

FRIED GREEN TOMATOES
Pomodori verdi fritti

Do you have green tomatoes left in the garden? You don't have to throw them away; there are good ways to use them, such as in this recipe. Also, refer to Chapter 1, Preserving, Pickling, and Freezing.

3 eggs
1 cup unflavored bread crumbs
½ teaspoon salt
¼ teaspoon black pepper
1 teaspoon marjoram
6 medium green tomatoes, cut into ¼-inch-thick slices
sweet butter or margarine, enough for frying

Beat eggs in a bowl.

In another bowl combine bread crumbs, salt, pepper, and marjoram; mix well.

Dip each slice of tomato into the beaten eggs, then into the bread crumbs; shake off any excess.

Melt butter in a heavy frying pan; fry tomatoes over medium heat, 2 minutes on each side, or until golden. Transfer over paper towels to dry. Keep warm as you continue frying. Serve hot.

STUFFED BAKED TOMATOES
Pomodori ripieni al forno

Preheat oven to 350°F.
- 6 large or 12 small tomatoes
- 1 10-ounce package frozen chopped spinach
- 3 tablespoons melted butter
- 6 tablespoons grated Parmesan or Asiago cheese
- 2 eggs, beaten
- ½ teaspoon salt
- 2 hard-cooked egg yolks, sieved

Remove ½ inch from top of each tomato; scoop out pulp and seeds (use for a sauce). Thaw spinach and drain well.

In a bowl combine spinach, butter, cheese, eggs, and salt; mix well. Fill tomato with spinach mixture. Place in a baking dish and bake for 30 minutes.

Remove from oven; transfer to a serving dish; garnish tomatoes with sieved egg yolks, and serve hot. Serves 6.

BAKED ZUCCHINI WITH PEPPERS AND TOMATOES
Zucchine, peperoni, pomodori al forno

Preheat oven to 350°F.
- 3 tablespoons butter
- 3 tablespoons oil
- 1 pound onions, sliced
- 3 medium zucchini, cut in ¼-inch slices
- 3 green peppers, cut in ½-inch strips
- 2 stalks celery, cut into 2-inch pieces
- 3 large sun-ripened tomatoes, or
- 4 canned plum tomatoes, chopped
- 1 teaspoon salt
- ½ teaspoon black pepper
- 4 leaves fresh basil

Melt butter in a large skillet; add oil. Sauté onions for 5 minutes; add remaining vegetables, salt, pepper, and basil.

Transfer to a well-oiled bake-and-serve casserole. Bake for 20 minutes. Serves 6.

BAKED ZUCCHINI WITH TOMATOES

Zucchine al forno con pomodori

Preheat oven to 350°F.

6	tablespoons corn oil
4	large fresh tomatoes, or
16	ounces canned plum tomatoes, drained
½	cup chopped fresh basil
1	clove garlic, minced
1	teaspoon salt
½	teaspoon black pepper
2½	pounds fresh zucchini, about 6 inches long
	oil for casserole
½	cup wheat germ

Heat 3 tablespoons oil in skillet; add tomatoes and sauté for 5 minutes over medium heat; stir in basil, garlic, salt, and pepper. Remove from heat; place in a bowl and set aside.

In the same skillet, heat remaining oil, and sauté zucchini for 5 minutes.

Oil well a bake-and-serve casserole; place tomato and zucchini in alternating layers; sprinkle top with wheat germ. Bake for 15 minutes. Serves 6.

FRIED ZUCCHINI WITH ALMONDS

Zucchine fritte con mandorle

1½	pounds fresh zucchini, about 6 to 8 inches long
2	tablespoons oil
2	tablespoons butter
¼	cup dry white wine
2	tablespoons lemon juice
½	teaspoon salt
½	cup slivered almonds

Wash and cut zucchini into ¼-inch slices; sauté slices in oil and butter for 5 minutes, stirring frequently. Add wine, lemon juice, and salt; simmer for 5 minutes; add almonds and simmer 5 minutes longer. Transfer to a warm serving dish and serve hot. Serves 6.

GRAND-MOTHER'S STUFFED ZUCCHINI

Zucchine ripiene della nonna

Preheat oven to 400°F.

- 10 fresh zucchini, about 7 to 8 inches long
- 4 tablespoons butter
- 1 large onion, sliced
- 4 tablespoons flour
- 1 cup hot milk
- ½ cup grated Parmesan or Asiago cheese
- 2 tablespoons chopped fresh parsley
- ½ teaspoon salt
- ¼ teaspoon nutmeg
- 5 *amaretti* (Italian macaroons), crumbled
- 5 egg yolks

Wash zucchini under cold water; remove both ends; cut crosswise into 2-inch sections. With vegetable corer, remove all pulp, being careful not to perforate outside skin. Chop pulp and set aside. Simmer hollowed-out zucchini in boiling salted water for 15 minutes. Drain and set aside.

In a saucepan, melt 3 tablespoons butter, and add onion. Cook over medium heat until onion turns golden; remove from saucepan. To butter remaining in saucepan, add flour and stir for 2 minutes; add hot milk and stir constantly, until sauce is creamy and thickened; mix in cheese, parsley, salt, nutmeg, amaretti, and egg yolks.

Stuff hollowed-out zucchini with the mixture; arrange in a buttered bake-and-serve dish; bake for 20 to 30 minutes. Serve hot or cold. Serves 6.

MARINATED ZUCCHINI ALLA PIEMONTESE

Zucchine sott'aceto alla Piemontese

- 3 pounds fresh zucchini, about 6 inches long
- 1 cup oil
- 1 large onion, sliced
- 1 stalk celery, cut into 1-inch pieces
- 2 cloves garlic, sliced
- 1 teaspoon salt
- ½ teaspoon white pepper
- 2 cups white wine vinegar
- 1 cup water

Wash zucchini; remove both ends; cut into strips 2 inches long, ¼ inch thick.

In a skillet, deep-fry zucchini in hot oil for 2 minutes. Remove and place in a bowl.

To prepare marinade pour off all but ½ cup of oil from skillet; sauté onion, celery, and garlic for 5 minutes or until onion is soft. Add salt, pepper, vinegar, and water; cover and simmer for 15 minutes. Pour hot marinade over zucchini; cool and refrigerate for at least 48 hours before serving.

Marinated zucchini will keep in the refrigerator for 1 week. Serves 6.

SAUTÉED ZUCCHINI
Zucchine in padella

One of the easiest and most delicious ways of preparing zucchini; very good with roast chicken, or lamb.

3 pounds fresh zucchini, about 6 inches long
2 tablespoons corn oil
3 tablespoons sweet butter or margarine
2 cloves garlic, mashed
1 teaspoon rosemary leaves
  salt
  pepper

Wash zucchini; remove ends and cut into ¼-inch-thick pieces, sliced across.

Heat oil in a skillet; add butter, garlic, and rosemary; stir and cook over medium heat until garlic is soft. Add zucchini and sauté for 5 minutes, shaking the skillet constantly. They should be cooked, but crisp. Remove garlic, taste for salt and pepper. Transfer to a warm serving bowl and serve hot. Serves 6.

ZUCCHINI PICKLED NEAPOLITAN

Zucchine a "scapece"

This is the way Neapolitans take zucchini to a picnic; you may prepare eggplants in the same manner.

4 pounds fresh zucchini, about 6 inches long
corn oil for frying
½ cup chopped fresh parsley
4 cloves garlic, sliced
1 cup corn oil
1 cup wine vinegar
½ teaspoon crushed red pepper
1 teaspoon salt

Wash zucchini; cut off ends; cut into 2-inch-long strips, ½-inch thick. Heat oil in skillet; fry zucchini for 2 minutes, a few at a time. Transfer to a bowl and continue until all the zucchini are fried.

Pour off the oil from skillet and discard, or save for some other use. Combine in skillet parsley, garlic, oil, vinegar, red pepper, and salt. Cook over medium heat for 5 minutes. Pour hot oil mixture over zucchini. Cover and refrigerate for at least 2 days before serving. Serve at room temperature. Serves 6.

SALADS
Insalate

BEAN SALAD WITH GREEN MAYONNAISE

Insalata di fagioli con maionese verde

Could also be used as an appetizer at the table, served on a bed of lettuce.

1 16-ounce can red kidney beans
1 16-ounce can white kidney beans
2 cloves garlic, minced
1 cup green mayonnaise (see recipe in Chapter 5, Sauces)

Drain the beans and rinse well in cold water; drain again. Transfer to a salad bowl.

Prepare green mayonnaise. Add garlic and mayonnaise to beans in bowl. Toss gently but thoroughly. Serve at room temperature. Serves 6 to 8.

FAVA BEAN AND CHEESE SALAD
Insalata di fave con formaggio pecorino

Makes a good appetizer or a luncheon dish; must be made with fresh fava beans.

- 4   pounds fresh fava beans, shelled and peeled
- 8   ounces Pecorino cheese or sharp Cheddar, diced
- ½   cup olive oil
- ½   teaspoon white pepper
- salt to taste

Shell fava beans; remove thin skin and wash. Drain well. Place in a salad bowl; add cheese, oil, and pepper. Toss gently. Taste for salt. Cover and set aside at room temperature for at least 1 hour before serving. Serves 6.

GREEN OR WAX BEAN SALAD ALLA PIEMONTESE
Insalata di fagiolini alla Piemontese

Very good in summer or winter, especially with barbecued meats.

- 2   pounds fresh green or wax beans
- 5   tablespoons olive oil
- 2   tablespoons wine vinegar
- ½   teaspoon salt
- ½   teaspoon black pepper
- 2   cloves garlic, minced
- 2   tablespoons chopped fresh basil (omit if you do not have fresh)
- 2   tablespoons chopped fresh parsley

Remove ends and strings from fresh beans. Cut into 2-inch pieces. Place in vegetable steamer with 1 inch salted water; cover and steam for 7 minutes, or until tender to your liking; drain and cool. Transfer to a salad bowl.

In a small bowl, mix oil, vinegar, salt, pepper, garlic, basil, and parsley. Pour over beans; toss gently and place in refrigerator for 1 hour before serving. Serves 6.

ITALIAN GREEN BEANS WITH MAYONNAISE

Taccole alla maionese

You may not often find the fresh Italian beans, but experience proves that the frozen variety is quite a good substitute.

20 ounces frozen Italian green beans
¾ cup homemade or commercial mayonnaise (see recipe for homemade, Chapter 5, Sauces)
3 tablespoons chopped pimiento
½ cup sliced water chestnuts (a favorite addition)
1 teaspoon dry mustard
  salt
  pepper

Cook beans according to package directions; drain well.

In a salad bowl combine mayonnaise, pimiento, water chestnuts, and mustard. Beat with wire whisk to mix well. Taste for salt and pepper. Add well-drained beans; toss gently until well coated. Cover and chill before serving. Serves 6.

BEETS AND CAULIFLOWER SALAD

Insalata di barbabietole e cavolfiore

1 pound fresh beets, or
16 ounces canned sliced beets, drained
1 small cauliflower, about 1 pound, or
10 ounces frozen cauliflower, defrosted, drained
1 teaspoon salt
1 medium onion, grated
2 tablespoons chopped fresh parsley
½ cup olive oil
2 tablespoons wine vinegar
4 tablespoons black pepper
  salt

Wash fresh unpeeled beets; place in vegetable steamer with 1 inch salted water. Cover and steam for 15 minutes, or until fork tender. Drain, cool, peel, and cut into ¼-inch-thick slices.

To prepare cauliflower, see recipe for Cauliflower with Bagna Caôda, Chapter 2.

In a small bowl, combine grated onion, chopped parsley, oil, vinegar, and pepper; beat with wire whisk to mix well.

Transfer cooked beets and cauliflower to a salad bowl; pour dressing over, and toss gently. Taste for salt and pepper. Chill for at least 30 minutes before serving. Serves 6.

RAW BROCCOLI SALAD
Insalata di broccoli crudi

1 medium bunch fresh broccoli, about 1½ to 2 pounds
1 medium sweet onion, cut into very thin rings
4 tablespoons olive oil
2 tablespoons wine vinegar
½ teaspoon salt
¼ teaspoon black pepper
1 clove garlic, minced
1 tablespoon chopped fresh chives

Discard outer broccoli leaves, remove stems, save for a vegetable soup. Dice. Transfer broccoli to a salad bowl, top with sliced onions.

In a small bowl mix oil, vinegar, salt, pepper, garlic, and chives. Pour over broccoli; toss gently and set aside at room temperature for at least 30 minutes before serving. Serves 6.

RED CABBAGE SALAD "TORINO"
Insalata di cavolo rosso "Torino"

Named after the city where I was born, partly for nostalgic reasons, but mostly because you will not find this salad in any other region of Italy. You may find this the best cabbage salad you have ever eaten.

1 large red cabbage, shredded
1 recipe Bagna Caôda (see recipe for Hot Anchovy-Garlic Dip, Chapter 5, Sauces)

Remove outer leaves from cabbage. Core and shred very thin; you may use a food processor. Soak cabbage in cold water for 30 minutes; rinse and drain very well.

Make sauce, and use only as much as you like as a salad dressing; the remainder you may enjoy with other raw vegetables.

Transfer cabbage to a salad bowl; spoon enough hot sauce over it. Toss well, and set aside at room temperature for at least 1 hour before serving. Serves 6 to 8.

SAVOY CABBAGE SALAD

Insalata di cavolo verza

1 large Savoy cabbage, shredded
1 cup homemade or commercial mayonnaise (see recipe for homemade in Chapter 5, Sauces)
4 tablespoons fresh lemon juice
1 tablespoon prepared mustard
½ teaspoon black pepper
  salt to taste
3 hard-cooked eggs, diced

Remove and discard outer leaves. Core and shred cabbage very thin. You may use a food processor. Soak shredded cabbage in cold water for 30 minutes; rinse and drain very well. Transfer to a salad bowl.

In a small bowl, combine mayonnaise, lemon juice, mustard, and pepper; mix well with wire whisk; taste for salt. Add diced eggs to cabbage, pour mayonnaise mixture over it. Toss well. Chill for at least 30 minutes before serving. Serves 6 to 8.

COOKED CAULIFLOWER SALAD

Insalata di cavolfiore cotto

1 cauliflower head, about 1½ pounds
1 cup homemade or commercial mayonnaise (see recipe for homemade in Chapter 5, Sauces), or
1 cup plain yogurt
2 tablespoons prepared mustard
1 teaspoon caraway seeds
  salt to taste
¼ teaspoon white pepper
3 tablespoons chopped fresh parsley

To prepare cauliflower, see recipe for Cauliflower with Bagna Caôda, Chapter 2. Set aside to cool.

In a small bowl, combine mayonnaise, mustard, caraway seeds, salt, pepper, and chopped parsley; mix well until blended. Transfer cauliflower to a salad bowl, pour dressing over it, and toss gently. Chill well before serving. Serves 6.

COOKED CELERY ROOT SALAD
Insalata di sedano-rapa

2	celery roots
½	cup water
½	cup vinegar
½	teaspoon marjoram
1	clove garlic, mashed
½	teaspoon salt
½	teaspoon white pepper
	lettuce leaves

Peel celery and slice very thin. Place in a saucepan with water, vinegar, marjoram, garlic, salt, and pepper. Bring to a boil, reduce heat, and simmer for 20 minutes or until celery is fork-tender. Cool in own liquid. Serve in individual small bowls lined with lettuce leaves. Serves 6.

RAW CELERY ROOT SALAD
Sedano-rapa con maionese

3	celery roots
2	lemons
1	cup mayonnaise (see recipe in Chapter 5, Sauces)
2	teaspoons capers
2	anchovy fillets

Peel celery roots, cut into julienne strips, and soak in cold water to which has been added the juice of 2 lemons, to prevent celery from turning brown.

Prepare mayonnaise.

Finely chop capers and anchovies; stir into mayonnaise.

Drain celery very well; if necessary pat dry with paper towels. Place in salad bowl, pour mayonnaise sauce over; toss. Set aside at room temperature until ready to use. Serves 6.

CELERY SALAD WITH ITALIAN PROSCIUTTO
Insalata di sedano con prosciutto

Could be served as a light main dish for a luncheon.

4   celery hearts
    lettuce leaves
5   tablespoons olive oil
4   ounces thinly sliced Italian prosciutto, cut into julienne strips
½   cup chopped olives of your choice
1   tablespoon wine or tarragon vinegar
1   teaspoon prepared mustard
    salt
    pepper

Wash celery hearts; drain and slice about ½ inch thick. Place in a salad bowl lined with lettuce leaves.

In a small frying pan, heat 2 tablespoons oil, add prosciutto, and sauté for 5 minutes. Remove from heat; add olives, remaining oil, vinegar, and mustard; mix well. Pour over sliced celery; toss, taste for salt and pepper. Cover, and set aside until serving time, no longer than 30 minutes. Serves 6.

CUCUMBER SALAD
Insalata di cetrioli

3   medium cucumbers
2   small red or Italian onions
2   tablespoons olive oil
4   tablespoons tarragon or white wine vinegar
2   tablespoons chopped fresh tarragon or mint
½   teaspoon salt
½   teaspoon white pepper

Remove skin and seed from cucumbers and slice very thin. Peel and slice onions into very thin rings. Place cucumbers and onions in a salad bowl.

Combine oil, vinegar, tarragon, salt, and pepper; beat to blend well. Pour over cucumbers and onions; toss, and chill before serving. Serves 6.

RAW DANDELION SALAD	1½ pounds young dandelion leaves
Insalata di girasoli	3 tablespoons olive oil
	1 tablespoon wine vinegar
	¼ teaspoon salt
	½ teaspoon white pepper
	2 hard-cooked eggs, chopped
	1 clove garlic, finely chopped
	4 anchovy fillets, chopped

Remove roots and tough stems from dandelions; wash in several changes of cold water. Drain well. Place in a large salad bowl.

In a small bowl, combine oil, vinegar, salt, pepper, eggs, garlic, and anchovies; mix well. Pour over dandelions; toss and serve immediately. Serves 6.

WILTED DANDELION SALAD	2 pounds fresh dandelions
Insalata di girasoli "appassiti"	8 slices bacon
	4 tablespoons wine vinegar
	4 anchovy fillets, chopped
	¼ teaspoon black pepper

Remove roots and tough stems from dandelions; wash in several changes of water. Drain well. Place in a warm salad bowl and set aside.

Cook bacon in a small frying pan until crisp. Remove from frying pan and crumble. Return crumbled bacon to frying pan with drippings; add vinegar, anchovies, and pepper. Stir over low heat until hot. Pour hot bacon mixture over dandelions, toss, and serve immediately. Serves 6.

LENTIL AND TOMATO SALAD
Insalata di lenticchie e pomodori

2 cups dried lentils, or
20 ounces canned lentils, drained
1 large sweet onion, thinly sliced
2 tablespoons chopped fresh parsley
1 tablespoon chopped fresh chives
½ cup olive oil
3 tablespoons wine vinegar
½ teaspoon salt
¼ teaspoon white pepper
4 large fresh tomatoes, sliced

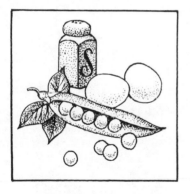

To prepare lentils, wash and drain. Place lentils in a saucepan; cover with water and bring to a boil. Cover pan and boil for 2 minutes. Remove from heat and let stand in water for at least 1 hour.

Drain lentils and transfer to a salad bowl. Add sliced onion, parsley, chives, oil, vinegar, salt, and pepper; toss gently and let stand at room temperature for at least 1 hour before serving. Arrange sliced tomatoes on top of lentils and serve. Serves 6.

RAW PEA SALAD WITH EGGS
Insalata di piselli freschi con uova

lettuce leaves
2 pounds fresh peas, shelled, washed, and well drained
4 hard-cooked eggs, chopped
5 tablespoons olive oil
2 tablespoons wine vinegar
½ teaspoon salt
½ teaspoon white pepper
½ to 1 teaspoon prepared mustard, according to your taste

Arrange lettuce leaves in individual salad bowls. Divide peas into bowls; top with some of the chopped eggs. Combine oil, vinegar, salt, pepper, and mustard; blend well. Just before serving sprinkle some dressing over each bowl. Serves 6.

POTATO AND MEAT SALAD

Insalata di patate con carne cotta

A good way to use leftover cooked beef or chicken. Very good for a summer meal.

6 medium potatoes
4 tablespoons white wine vinegar
3 tablespoons dry white wine
8 tablespoons olive oil
1 teaspoon prepared mustard
1 teaspoon dried tarragon leaves
1 teaspoon salt
½ teaspoon black pepper
1 large sweet onion, thinly sliced
2 cups diced cooked beef or chicken (good roast or boiled) lettuce leaves

Cook the potatoes (with their skins) in boiling salted water for 25 minutes, or until tender but firm. Drain and peel while warm. Cut into slices ¼ inch thick, and place in a salad bowl.

In a small bowl, combine vinegar, wine, oil, mustard, tarragon, salt, and pepper. Beat with a wire whisk until well mixed. Pour over potatoes; toss gently; cover and set aside at room temperature for at least 30 minutes.

Add sliced onion and diced meat; toss again. Transfer to a lettuce-lined salad bowl and serve. Serves 6.

WILTED SOYBEAN SPROUT SALAD
Insalata appassiti di germogli di soia

A variation of wilted spinach salad; try it, you may like it.

4 slices bacon, diced
1 pound soybean sprouts
3 scallions, thinly sliced
1½ cups cut green beans, cooked and drained
3 tablespoons corn oil
1 teaspoon flour
¼ cup white vinegar
3 tablespoons water
salt
pepper

Cook bacon in frying pan until crisp. Remove bacon pieces and set aside. In the same frying pan heat the sprouts, scallions, and beans for 5 minutes over medium heat, stirring constantly. Transfer to a salad bowl.

In a small saucepan, combine oil, flour, vinegar, water, salt, and pepper to taste. Bring to a boil. Pour over sprout mixture. Toss gently and sprinkle with bacon pieces. Cover and set aside in warm place for at least 30 minutes before serving. Serves 6.

SOYBEAN SPROUT SALAD
Insalata di germogli di soia

1 pound soybean sprouts
3 tablespoons ketchup
3 tablespoons mayonnaise
3 tablespoons sour cream
2 tablespoons fresh lemon juice
1 tablespoon chopped fresh parsley
¼ teaspoon cayenne pepper
salt to taste

Wash sprouts well; drain and transfer to a salad bowl.

In a small bowl, combine ketchup, mayonnaise, sour cream, lemon juice, parsley, pepper, and salt. Mix well with a wire whisk. Taste for additional salt and pepper. Pour over sprouts; toss and serve. Serves 6.

TOMATO, EGG, AND HERB SALAD

Insalata di pomodori

6   medium sun-ripened tomatoes
3   hard-cooked eggs, diced
2   bunches green onions or scallions, sliced
5   tablespoons oil
3   tablespoons wine vinegar
2   tablespoons chopped fresh parsley
2   tablespoons chopped fresh basil
1   teaspoon salt
¼   teaspoon black pepper

If you prefer, you can peel the tomatoes, but it is not necessary. Slice them into a salad bowl; add eggs and scallions; combine oil and vinegar and pour over; sprinkle with parsley, basil, salt, and pepper. Toss gently; cover and refrigerate for 2 or 3 hours. Serve chilled. Serves 6.

TOMATO, EGG, AND ANCHOVY SALAD

Insalata di pomodori uova, e acciughe

6   large ripe tomatoes, sliced
1   large sweet onion, sliced into thin rings
3   celery stalks, cut into ½-inch pieces
3   hard-cooked eggs, sliced
4   anchovy fillets, diced
½   teaspoon salt
3   tablespoons wine vinegar
2   teaspoons prepared mustard
¼   teaspoon white pepper
8   tablespoons olive oil
2   teaspoons caraway seeds

Place sliced tomatoes in a salad bowl; spread onions, celery, eggs, and anchovies over tomatoes.

In a small bowl combine salt with vinegar, then add mustard and pepper; stir in oil and caraway seeds; stir with a wire whisk to mix well. Pour over tomatoes, toss gently, and serve. Serves 6.

FRESH ZUCCHINI SALAD
Insalata di zucchine

You must use very fresh and very small zucchini for this salad.

12 very small fresh zucchini, about 4 inches long
    juice from 2 lemons, strained
½   teaspoon salt
½   teaspoon white pepper
2   tablespoons chopped fresh mint
6   tablespoons olive oil

Place zucchini in a bowl; add ice cubes and cover with water; refrigerate for at least 2 hours before preparing salad. This will make the zucchini crisp.

In a small bowl, combine lemon juice, salt, pepper, mint, and oil; beat with wire whisk to mix well. Taste for additional salt or pepper.

Dry zucchini well with paper towels; remove both ends. Cut into very thin slices and place in salad bowl. Pour dressing over; toss very gently and serve immediately. Serves 6.

9 Desserts
Cakes Breads

Dolci: Torte, pane

CAKES
Torte

**BUTTERNUT
SQUASH
SQUARES**

Dolcetti di zucca

Preheat oven to 325°F.

4	tablespoons sweet butter or margarine
1	cup brown sugar
3	eggs
3	cups cooked, mashed Butternut squash
2½	cups flour
2	teaspoons baking powder
½	teaspoon salt
¼	teaspoon cloves
¼	teaspoon nutmeg
1	teaspoon cinnamon
1½	cups seedless raisins
1	cup chopped almonds

Combine 3 tablespoons butter and sugar in a large bowl and cream well with an electric mixer; add eggs one at a time and beat well after each addition. Stir in squash and beat for 1 minute. Combine flour with baking powder, salt, cloves, nutmeg, and cinnamon; mix well. Add to squash and mix for 3 minutes. Stir in raisins and almonds.

Pour batter into a well-buttered 13 × 9 × 2-inch baking pan. Bake for 15 minutes, or until an inserted knife comes out clean. Cool in pan on wire rack. Cut into squares before serving. Makes 15 squares.

CARROT BARS
Biscotti di carote

This is the best way to get children to eat carrots; it worked with my son.

Preheat oven to 350°F.

 8 tablespoons melted sweet butter or margarine
 1 cup honey
 2 eggs
 4 tablespoons melted semisweet chocolate
 2 cups flour
 2 teaspoons baking powder
 ½ teaspoon salt
 2 cups finely grated fresh carrots
 1 teaspoon almond extract
 ½ cup chopped walnuts or pecans
    oil for baking pan

In a bowl, combine melted butter with honey and mix well. Beat in eggs one at a time, add chocolate; beat well. Add flour, baking powder, salt, carrots, almond extract, and walnuts. Beat until well blended. Pour mixture into a well-oiled 9 × 9-inch baking pan and bake for 25 minutes. Turn out and cut into bars. Makes about 30 bars.

CARROT CUSTARD
Budino di carote

Preheat oven to 300°F.

1½ cups cooked, mashed carrots
½ cup brown sugar
½ teaspoon cloves
½ teaspoon cinnamon
⅛ teaspoon nutmeg
   pinch salt
3 eggs
1½ cups light cream, or
1 cup evaporated skim milk plus 2 tablespoons nonfat dry milk
½ cup slivered almonds
   butter for custard cups

In a large bowl, combine mashed carrots, sugar, cloves, cinnamon, nutmeg, and salt, and mix well with a wire whisk. Add eggs, one at a time, and mix well after each addition. Add cream and mix well. Pour mixture into 6 well-buttered custard cups; sprinkle top with some of the slivered almonds. Place cups in a shallow baking pan, and pour boiling water into the pan to come at least halfway up the side of cups.

Bake for 1 hour, or until an inserted knife comes out clean. Transfer cups from pan to wire rack to cool. Serve warm or chilled. Serves 6.

CARROT OR PUMPKIN PUDDING
Budino dolce di carote o zucca

Preheat oven to 325°F.

4 cups cooked, mashed carrots or pumpkin
5 tablespoons melted sweet butter or margarine
¼ cup brown sugar
4 eggs, beaten
1 teaspoon grated fresh orange rind
¼ cup orange liqueur
1 cup fine crumbs *amaretti* (Italian macaroons)

In a bowl, combine mashed carrots with 4 tablespoons melted butter, and sugar; add eggs and mix well. Stir in orange rind and orange liqueur.

Butter a 1½-quart baking dish, sprinkle with ½ cup of crumbs. Pour in carrot mixture and sprinkle top with remaining crumbs. Bake for 1 hour. Good warm or cold. Serves 6.

CARROT ICE CREAM SQUARES
Dolcetti di carote con gelato

1	cup fine crumbs *amaretti* (Italian macaroons)
3	tablespoons brown sugar
4	tablespoons melted sweet butter or margarine
2	tablespoons unflavored gelatin
½	cup cold water
1	cup cooked, mashed carrots
¼	teaspoon salt
1½	teaspoons cinnamon
2	teaspoons almond extract or Amaretto liqueur
1	quart chocolate or vanilla ice cream
½	cup sliced almonds

In a small bowl, combine amaretti crumbs with sugar and melted butter; mix well. Reserve ¼ cup of crumbs mixture. Press remaining crumbs into bottom of 8 × 8-inch baking pan. Sprinkle gelatin into cold water; stir to soften.

In a saucepan, combine carrots, salt, cinnamon, and almond extract; stir in gelatin. Place over low heat and stir until gelatin is dissolved. Set aside to cool.

Chill a large bowl; place ice cream in bowl and stir until softened; gently fold in carrot mixture.

Spoon ice cream/carrot mixture over crust in pan. Combine reserved crumbs with almonds and sprinkle over top. Cover and place in the freezer for at least 4 hours. Cut into squares before serving. Makes 16 squares.

CAULIFLOWER CAKE

Torta di cavolfiore

Another trick for little vegetable haters.

Preheat oven to 350°F.

   8 tablespoons sweet butter or margarine
   1 cup honey
   3 eggs
   1 teaspoon vanilla extract
   ½ cup unsweetened cocoa
   2½ cups flour
   1 teaspoon baking powder
   1 teaspoon baking soda
     pinch salt
   1 cup chopped fresh cauliflower
   ½ cup chopped walnuts
     oil for baking pan

In a large bowl, cream butter with honey using an electric mixer; add eggs and vanilla and beat until fluffy. Stir in cocoa, flour, baking powder, baking soda, salt, cauliflower, and walnuts; beat for 5 minutes, or until well blended.

Spoon mixture into a well-oiled tube cake pan. Bake for 30 minutes, or until an inserted knife comes out clean. Turn cake onto a wire rack to cool. Serves 10.

FENNEL CAKE

Torta di finocchi

Preheat oven to 350°F.

   2 medium fennels
   2½ cups flour
   1¼ cups sugar, or
   1 cup honey
   ¼ teaspoon baking powder
   1½ teaspoons baking soda
   1 teaspoon vanilla extract
   2 teaspoons grated fresh lemon rind
   4 tablespoons shortening, at room temperature
   3 eggs
   1 teaspoon salt
   1 cup chopped walnuts
     oil for baking pan

To prepare fennels, remove tops and tough outer leaves. Dice fennels, and rinse well. Place in vegetable steamer with 1 teaspoon salt; cover and steam for 20 minutes. Drain, and transfer to the container of an electric blender or food processor and puree. Set aside.

Sift together flour, sugar (if using honey, add to mixture after you add fennel puree), baking powder, and baking soda, all into a large mixing bowl. Add vanilla, lemon rind, shortening and fennel puree; beat with electric beater until just blended. Add eggs and beat at medium speed for 2 minutes; add salt. Fold in walnuts by hand.

Spoon batter into a well-greased 13 × 9 × 2-inch baking pan. Bake for 45 minutes, or until an inserted knife comes out clean. Cool cake in pan. Serves 6 to 8.

PUMPKIN CAKE
Torta di zucca

This cake freezes well.

Preheat oven to 350°F.

3	eggs
1½	cups sugar, or
1	cup honey
1	cup corn oil (if using honey, use only ¾ cup of oil)
½	teaspoon cinnamon
½	teaspoon ginger
¼	teaspoon cloves
¼	teaspoon nutmeg
2½	teaspoons baking soda
1	teaspoon salt
2	teaspoons baking powder
2	cups flour
2½	cups cooked and pureed pumpkin (you may use canned pumpkin)
1	cup chopped walnuts or pecans
½	cup seedless raisins, soaked and drained
	oil for baking pan

In a large mixing bowl beat eggs with sugar until eggs are lemon-colored and frothy. Add oil, cinnamon, ginger, cloves, nutmeg, baking soda, salt, baking powder, and flour; beat to mix well. Fold in the pumpkin, walnuts, and raisins.

Pour mixture into a well-greased and floured tube pan. Bake for 55 minutes, or until an inserted knife comes out clean. Cool in pan for 10 minutes, then invert with pan on a wire rack. Cool completely before removing pan. Serves 12.

SWEET POTATO PUDDING

Budino di patate dolci

Preheat oven to 350°F.

 2 pounds sweet potatoes or yams
 1 pound Delicious apples
 ½ teaspoon salt
 7 tablespoons melted sweet butter or margarine
 1 cup honey
 ½ cup dry Marsala or port wine

Peel sweet potatoes and cut into ¼-inch-thick slices. Peel and cut apple the same way.

In a small bowl, combine salt, 6 tablespoons butter, honey, and wine; mix well.

Arrange potatoes and apples in alternate layers in a well-buttered bake-and-serve casserole. Pour some of the honey mixture between each layer. Cover. Bake for 30 minutes. Serve hot. Serves 6.

SWEET POTATO SOUFFLÉ

Sformato di patate dolci

Preheat oven to 300°F.

 2 cups cooked mashed sweet potatoes or yams
 2 tablespoons brown sugar
 ½ teaspoon salt
 2 eggs, separated
 ¼ cup Amaretto liqueur
 4 tablespoons seedless raisins
   butter for baking pan

In a bowl, combine mashed potatoes, sugar, salt, egg yolks, and liqueur; mix well. Beat egg whites until peaks form; fold gently into potato mixture; fold in raisins.

Pour mixture into a well-buttered 1-quart soufflé dish. Bake for 45 minutes, or until firm. Serve immediately. Serves 6.

ZUCCHINI CHOCOLATE CAKE

Torta di zucchine al cioccolato

Preheat oven to 350°F.

3	ounces bitter chocolate, melted
3½	cups flour
1½	teaspoons baking powder
2	teaspoons baking soda
1	teaspoon salt
4	eggs
1	cup sugar or
1½	cups honey
2	teaspoons vanilla extract
2	cups corn oil
4	fresh zucchini, about 7 inches long, grated
1	cup chopped walnuts or pecans

Melt chocolate, and set aside to cool.

Sift together flour, baking powder, baking soda, and salt. Set aside.

In a large mixing bowl, beat eggs with sugar and honey until creamy and light in color; add vanilla, 1½ cups oil, and cooled, melted chocolate; beat until well blended. Stir in flour mixture a little at a time, beating after each addition until well blended. Add grated zucchini and walnuts; stir well.

Pour batter into a well-oiled and floured tube cake pan. Bake for 1 hour and 15 minutes, or until an inserted knife comes out clean. Cool in pan on wire rack for 10 minutes. Remove from pan and cool completely on wire rack. Serves 12.

BREADS
Pane

**ACORN SQUASH
BREAD**
Pane di zucca

In Italy you do not find Acorn squash, but from a similar squash used there I have adapted an excellent recipe.

Preheat oven to 350°F.

    1 cup honey
1½ cups Acorn squash, cooked and mashed, or
 10 ounces canned pumpkin
  6 tablespoons melted sweet butter or margarine
  2 eggs
  2 cups flour
1½ teaspoons baking soda
½ teaspoon nutmeg
½ teaspoon cinnamon
  1 cup seedless raisins
½ cup chopped almonds
    oil for baking pan

Combine in a mixing bowl honey, squash, melted butter, and eggs; beat until well blended. Stir in flour, baking soda, nutmeg, and cinnamon; mix well. Add raisins and almonds and stir.

Turn out into a well-greased and floured 9-inch bread loaf pan. Bake for 1 hour and 15 minutes, or until inserted knife comes out clean. Makes 1 loaf.

ARTICHOKE BREAD
Pane con carciofi

Different, but good.

Preheat oven to 350°F.
- 1 cup light brown sugar
- 4 tablespoons sweet butter or margarine
- 3 tablespoons yogurt
- 1 teaspoon baking soda
- ½ teaspoon baking powder
- ¼ teaspoon salt
- 1½ cups mashed artichoke hearts, frozen or canned, defrosted and drained
- ½ cup chopped walnuts or pecans
- ½ teaspoon cinnamon
- ⅛ teaspoon nutmeg
- 1¾ cups whole wheat flour
- 2 egg whites
  oil for baking pan

With electric mixer cream sugar and butter until smooth; add yogurt, baking soda, baking powder, salt, artichoke hearts, pecans, cinnamon, nutmeg, and flour; beat until well mixed. Beat egg white until peaks form, fold gently into flour mixture.

Pour into well-greased loaf pan or tube cake pan. Bake for 1 hour. Serves 6 to 10.

BEAN BREAD
Pane di fagioli

Makes a robust loaf of bread; all you need is some cheese, and you have a walk-in-the-woods snack.

Preheat oven to 350°F.

1	cup warm, cooked, mashed dried red kidney beans, or
16	ounces canned kidney beans, drained
4	tablespoons sweet butter or margarine, at room temperature
1	cup honey
1	egg, beaten
¾	cup whole wheat flour
1	teaspoon salt
1	teaspoon cinnamon
½	teaspoon nutmeg
¼	teaspoon cloves
1½	teaspoons baking soda
2	cups apple sauce
½	teaspoon chopped walnuts or pecans

Wash beans thoroughly. Place beans in a bowl and cover with water. Soak overnight. Or, boil beans for 3 minutes, remove from heat, cover pot and let stand for 2 hours. Drain. Transfer soaked beans to a saucepan; cover with hot water plus 2 inches. Cover pan; bring to a boil; reduce heat and cook for 1½ to 2 hours, or until beans are tender. Drain. Place beans in container of an electric blender or food processor and puree thoroughly. Keep warm.

Place butter in a large mixing bowl. Add honey, and beat until well blended. Add pureed beans, beaten egg, and blend well with electric beater. Stir in flour, salt, cinnamon, nutmeg, cloves, and baking soda; mix well. Add apple sauce and walnuts; mix.

Spoon mixture into a tube cake pan or a loaf pan. Bake for 1 hour, or until an inserted knife comes out clean. Cool bread in pan for 20 minutes before cooling completely on wire cake rack. Serves 10 to 12.

ONION AND CHEESE BREAD

Pane con cipolle e formaggio

Very good for a *merenda* (afternoon snack), or a picnic.

Preheat oven to 350°F.
- 3 tablespoons corn oil
- 1 cup finely chopped onions
- 1 cup softened margarine
- 1 egg
- 1 cup grated Swiss cheese
- 2 cups flour
- 3 tablespoons baking powder
- ¼ teaspoon salt
- ½ cup milk

Heat 2 tablespoons oil in frying pan; add onions; sauté over high heat until golden and crisp. Drain on paper towels. Set aside.

In a bowl, combine margarine with egg; beat until well creamed; add cheese and onions and mix well.

Combine flour with baking powder and salt; add to onion mixture alternately with the milk; mix well. If dough is too dry, add a little more milk.

Turn mixture into a well-greased 9 × 5-inch loaf pan. Bake for 45 to 50 minutes, or until an inserted knife comes out clean. Cool on wire rack. Makes 1 loaf.

ZUCCHINI-OAT BREAD

Pane d'avena con zucchine

Preheat oven to 350°F.
- 1 cup honey
- 3 eggs
- ⅔ cup corn oil
- 1 teaspoon almond extract
- 2½ cups flour
- 1 cup rolled oats, quick cooking or old-fashioned
- 2 teaspoons baking powder
- 1 teaspoon baking soda
- 2 teaspoons cinnamon
- 1½ teaspoons salt
- ½ teaspoon nutmeg
- 4 fresh zucchini, about 7 inches long, shredded
- 1 cup chopped almonds

In a mixing bowl, with an electric mixer, beat honey with eggs, until light in color; add oil, and almond extract; beat for 2 minutes.

Combine flour, oats, baking powder, baking soda, cinnamon, salt, and nutmeg. Add to honey mixture and mix until just dry. Stir in zucchini and almonds.

Spoon batter into two 9 × 5-inch loaf pans. Bake for 50 minutes or until an inserted knife comes out clean. Cool in pans for 10 minutes. Remove from pan and cool completely on wire racks. Makes 2 loaves.

Index

About the Author

The daughter of Italian restaurateurs, Teresa Gilardi Candler came to America in 1953. She is a food editor and author of a syndicated food column "From Teresa's Kitchen." She is also a consultant to food companies and restaurants, and a photo stylist. Author of *The Northern Italian Cookbook*, she lives with her family in Closter, New Jersey.